mortician diaries

mortician diaries

the dead-honest truth from a life spent with death

June Knights Nadle

New World Library
Novato, California

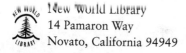
New World Library
14 Pamaron Way
Novato, California 94949

Cover design by Laura Beers
Interior design by Madonna Gauding

PUBLISHER CATALOGING-IN-PUBLICATION DATA
Nadle, June Knights.
Mortician diaries : the dead-honest truth from a life spent with death
/ June Knights Nadle.
p. cm.
ISBN: 978-1-973072-62-0
1. Undertakers and undertaking--Miscellanea. 2. Death--
Psychological aspects. 3. Death--Social aspects. I. Title.
HQ1073 .N33 2006
363.7/5--dc22 0608

First printing, May 2006
ISBN: 978-1-973072-62-0

10 9 8 7 6 5 4 3 2

Dedicated to my husband
Edward A. Nadle
1912–2001

Acknowledgements

I appreciate the families who gave their permission for me to tell their stories in the hope it might help others who find themselves in similar circumstances.

Many thanks to my agent, Lorin Rees, of the Helen Rees Agency in Boston. Upon receiving my stories he said, "I think you have something here." Then thanks to Alma Bune of Inner Ocean Publishing who agreed with Lorin after other editors said, "Death won't sell." Alma sent Angela Watrous to me to give tremendous editorial help to this mortician who wanted to tell her stories.

My gratitude to my second husband, Ed, who used reverse psychology by saying to me in 1983, "You'll never write that book." But I did. Then in 2001, after serving as my major critic for eight years, he said, "I won't live to see your book published." He didn't.

I extend my thanks to those who went the extra mile to assist me: Jean Cruickshank, Cathy Hoyt, Josh Sens, Jacquelyn Hurst, Dawn Sandberg, Douglas and Corine Parker, Ron Broomhead, Nonna Kocharyan, Angela Graham, Rebecca Newman of UCLA, my family of Hamiltons (my maiden name), and Ed's grandchildren who cheered me on. I was learning to use a computer when my actor friend, Johnny Mask, read the manuscript and said, "Great stories. Now turn on your spell checker, girl."

To the fourteen members of a book club I belong to, who read for me, gave me feedback, and asked questions, I give a great big THANK YOU!

Contents

Introduction

We understand death for the first time
When he puts his hand upon one whom we love.
—Madame de Staël

When people meet me, they often have a hard time reconciling who I am with what I do. I am an eighty-year-old grandmother with silver hair, a "sweet old lady" to the average eye. But I am also a mortician: a funeral director, an undertaker, a servant in the death care industry.

I got started in the business in my early twenties, just after World War II, in an era when most women had few career options. Schoolteacher. Secretary. Nurse. I chose mortuary work instead.

For the next fifty years, I worked mostly in Los Angeles and Salt Lake City. My employers ranged from mom-and-pop mortuaries to a large company regarded as the Wal-Mart of funeral homes. My clientele cut across a broad swath of humanity: the poor and the fabulously wealthy; misers, magistrates, and misanthropes; newborn babies and octogenarians. All races, colors, and creeds.

My work has taught me that one thing in life is certain: The death rate in the world is one per person.

If you are like most people, your awareness of what must come is coupled with a deep reluctance to confront it. Maybe you've penned a will or even purchased a cemetery plot. But chances are you haven't yet tackled the most important and rewarding task: engaging in a dialogue on death.

A dialogue on death

I first came across that phrase in the writings of Dr. Scott Peck, a physician, philosopher, and theologian well regarded for his work on the link between spirituality and well-being. In his book, *Denial of the Soul,* Dr. Peck relayed the story of a popular high school student who was killed in a car crash. Three days later, another student at the same school died of leukemia. The classmates of the dead teens were traumatized and confused. They appealed to their principal to create a class that would help them learn how to deal with death. They even found a minister who offered to teach the class for free. But when the principal asked the school board for permission, his request was shot down. Death, the board decided, was too morbid a subject to teach in school.

Dr. Peck told the story as a lament. He urged us to deal more directly with death—to contemplate it seriously (without obsessing) and talk about it openly with the ones we love.

He referred to it as a dialogue on death. His words struck a cord with me.

I decided to write this book to help readers get started with their own dialogue on death—which can ultimately have great impact on how we chose to live our lives. When we don't live in awareness about death's inevitability, its finality brings with it so many wishes and regrets. In the course of my career, the words I've heard more often than any others are, *I wish*. "I wish we had taken the trip to Ireland we always planned." "I wish I had kissed him on the morning he had the accident." "I wish I had been kinder." "I wish I hadn't lied." If only those clients had engaged in a dialogue on death, perhaps they could have identified what was really important to them before it was too late.

A dialogue on death doesn't have to be a downer. Actually, it can be downright uplifting. In my experience, talking about death openly, honestly, intimately, brings us closer to friends and loved ones. It promotes kindness in relationships. It helps us appreciate the time we have.

Throughout my career, as I witnessed so many tragedies of words unspoken, dreams unfulfilled, and relationships unmended, it gradually changed how I looked at life. Kind words shouldn't go unspoken, nor should the sweet gesture go unfulfilled. Wishes should not rot into regrets. I learned about avoiding unnecessary pain. In going through my own divorce and raising a severely disabled child, I saw that living life inherently brings its own pain, without my needing to add to it with unresolved complaints and grudges. I learned that there is no taking back the past, and that death often comes when we least expect it.

Over the years, I have often been asked to speak to church and civic groups and university classes about my professional experiences. After one such talk, a woman from the audience stood up. "I really want to talk about what I want done when I die," she said, "but both my daughters say it's too morbid and they don't want to talk about it."

I suggested she tell them they were both disinherited if they didn't talk with her. I was joking, of course, and the audience laughed. Still, I told the woman, in all seriousness (and it's the same thing I'll tell you now) that everyone benefits when you deal openly and realistically with death. First, take care of the pragmatics: Write a will. Make your final arrangements. Make your wishes clear. And make them known to those you love. I've heard men say, "Just put me in a wooden box and bury me in the backyard." There isn't a widow in the world who would do that (never mind that it's illegal). You owe it to yourself and the ones you love to take this responsibility seriously.

Of course, that is only the beginning of your personal dialogue on death. It's my hope that the stories in this book, recounting some of the most compelling and poignant deaths that I've encountered in my professional and personal experiences, will incite your own realizations about how you want to relate to life and death. Early on in my writing, I began sharing my manuscript in progress with various acquaintances, including my plumber. When I ran into him in town a few weeks later, he said, with a touch of amazement, "What have you done to my wife? She wouldn't put those stories down, and she just cried and cried. And she never cries, not when we lost our baby when we were young, not when her mother was killed so many years back. She just closed up, unreachable, and now all of a sudden she's talking about it."

Later that week, I got an email from his wife: "I am a stuffer; I stuff my feelings and emotions down inside me so I don't have to deal with them. My mother has been gone for twelve years and I still haven't dealt with some of her matters. Reading your stories has brought some of my feelings to the surface and I hope I can use this time to move forward."

I knew I was on the right track, that the stories were speaking to people as they'd spoken to me over the years.

The nature of each of our internal dialogues with death will vary, but hopefully the stories in this book can lead you into this uncharted territory. I don't have all the answers, but repetition can be a good teacher, so I'm well-practiced in the realities of death. These stories are a compilation of some of the most illuminating experiences of my career. Some are funny. Some are sad. Some haunt me with their strangeness. In them you will see the many ways people cope with death. And hopefully, after reading about the successes and struggles of these families, you will begin to think clearly about your own relationship with death.

People often ask me if mortuary work is morbid or depressing. "Neither," I respond. "Most of my time is spent with the living." Same with this book. It is for the living, not for those who have passed on. By sharing my experiences, I hope to help you find some measure of comfort with what every life must bring.

Above all, this book on death is a guide to really living life.

Chapter One

Acknowledging the Inevitable

Mortician's Diary

I was born and raised in southeastern Idaho on a small farm. We grew potatoes in the valley and Dad raised sheep in the mountains of Wyoming.

I used to hang around the lambing corrals while my father and the other men worked. When a mother ewe is ready to "drop," or give birth, she is placed in a small pen so that she and her new offspring can be observed. If the birth goes well and mother and baby have no trouble bonding (every now and then, a free-spirited ewe decides she'd rather not be bothered by the trials of motherhood and rejects her lamb), the pair is moved to a pen with ten others, where they spend a few days getting used to being with other sheep. At that point they join a larger group of fifty or so ewes. This happens again and again until a herd of some one thousand ewes has been assembled and is ready to hit the open range.

Rejected or orphaned lambs are known as "bum lambs" and my younger brother, Rex, and I raised around fifty of them each year. We used large root beer bottles full of milk with oversized nipples we purchased at the drug store for a nickel. The lambs were an ambitious lot. They often knocked us down in a mad dash for their food. We soon learned to put the nipple through the wire fence, but it was difficult to take the bottle from one lamb and give it to another. The chronically famished little creatures climbed over and under each other in their battle to be the first to latch onto the nipple. They never seemed to have enough milk even though their bellies bulged.

I discovered one year that it wasn't wise to make pets of them. Although my name is not Mary, I had a little lamb that followed me everywhere I went. I loved her and she loved ice cream, so every day I shared my ice cream with her. Then came August and it was time for her to be sold off to become someone's dinner. As she was loaded on a freight car headed for Chicago, I couldn't help but think about how the ice cream I'd fed her had prepared her all-too-well for the market.

Farm life teaches you a lot about the realities of life and death. When I was nine years old, I had a tortoiseshell cat named Tabby who brought many lessons into my life. Tortoiseshells are always female and usually mild mannered. Their fur is patterned with small patches of brown, orange, black, and gray. Every night at bedtime, Tabby would push open the screen of my bedroom window, crawl under the covers, put her head next to mine on the pillow, and purr me to sleep. She exited the same way every morning when she heard my parents stirring downstairs, as if she knew they disapproved of farm animals in the house.

At some point Tabby became pregnant, and near her delivery time she settled into a clean corner of our coal shed. I put pieces of old blankets down for her bed. When she didn't appear for breakfast one day, I went to her bed and found her in the throes of labor. Her whole body seemed to spasm with each labor pain, and she reached for my hand with her paw. I sat by Tabby until the afternoon, but still she had not produced a kitten. She would grasp my hand with her bare claws as the pains came. I summoned Mother and she applied gentle pressure in two or three places before announcing that a kitten was coming breech. She told me I could very gently and slowly pull on the end of the kitten to help Tabby. Then Mom returned to the house.

I eased the birth by pulling gently on the kitten's tail, and when it finally came out it was obviously stillborn. In a few minutes a live kitten came and I helped to clean it up with a piece of toweling. Then a deformed kitten presented itself and breathed only a minute or so before dying. All of this birth and death happened in a few minutes. There was little need for the birds-and-bees lecture for those of us raised around animals.

After that Tabby and I had two wonderful years together, during which she was playful and cuddly. Then she started to lose her appetite and sleep a lot. Her loss of weight was noticeable, but on the farm no one ever thought of a veterinarian for any animal except horses and cows. Small animals that became ill or maimed were usually shot. It was neither cruel nor kind. It just was. Still, I asked Dad not to shoot Tabby when she became obviously too ill to recover. He agreed and I held her while she died. Yes, my heart was broken, but Dad helped me bury her.

While I was sad at losing my pet, I was grateful I could care for her and hold her to the end. That way, I didn't have to wonder about how she died. I didn't need to worry that another animal had disturbed her. I knew she had comfort from being in my arms. I felt a peace in my own mind by staying. Years later when I was with my husband in his passing, that same peace came to me.

In living around animals, death is always a possibility. My dad took me to the pasture after a big lightning storm. Lightning had killed two cows and a calf. Dad showed me the jagged lines of burned grass and torn sod next to the bodies. Another time, I was with my older brother in the mountains when he shot and killed a sleek, fat mountain lion. The lion was beautiful, but it had acquired its fat by killing and eating our sheep. Our sheep represented our livelihood. The lion had to go. Nature seemed pretty cruel sometimes, but seeing these deaths taught me that it was an inescapable and inevitable thing about life.

Sometimes, people in my life died, too. When my grandfather passed away, his body was returned to his home to stay for a twenty-four-hour period—something very common in those days. I watched through the banister of the stairway as the grown-ups talked and even sang as they sat in a semicircle around the casket all through the night. The reality of death was indelibly etched on my mind. It was a very real, very conscious part of my life.

I do not remember that my parents ever made a point of teaching me specifically about death. They simply took my hand and led me to any occasion that involved our family. Times were different four generations ago. Our relatives lived near us and we gathered frequently. Just as the corporations have taken over many mom-and-pop mortuaries, so too have the conglomerates taken over farms, so few children have the same learning opportunities I did.

In the process of writing this book, I handed a copy of the stories I had assembled to a friend who has three teenage daughters. After reading the manuscript, she asked her husband to read it. Then they gave the stories to their daughters. After that, they sat down and talked about the stories and their own ideas about death and funerals. They invited me to dinner to thank me for raising their awareness and giving them the chance to change some of their actions and attitudes. They said the stories helped them start to see death as a very natural life experience.

I do not remember any time that death seemed strange to me. I do not have any recollection of being afraid of it. It just was. However, when I decided on a career in the death care industry, it was the service aspect of it that appealed to me. I had watched the funeral directors at work and they always appeared to be helping people. I liked offering support to families in need. It's my hope that I can offer a similar kind of help by sharing these stories with you.

The Spitfire Who Planned Her Own Funeral

I met Lucy when I joined a study group for seniors. Lucy was in her mid-seventies. She had white wavy hair and hardly a wrinkle in her face, and her sense of humor made me like her immediately. As we became acquainted she confessed that her newest friend was a funeral director named Wally, whom she met when she went to the local funeral home to talk about arrangements for her own funeral and burial. The experience she described was fun and funny.

She picked out her casket and gave him a suggested order of service, which was to be held in the mortuary chapel. She wanted everyone who came to have a good time. Only laughter would be allowed and her four sons and four grandchildren were to present the program. Her funeral was to be a celebration. She planned to be interred in the grave next to her husband in the local cemetery.

When they were finished making arrangements, she told Wally she admired his neat comb-over. Then she paid him and promised to bring her burial clothing the next week to be placed in their "future" closet—just as soon as she found the brightest red dress in town.

During the next two years that I knew her, Lucy just enjoyed life. Then everything changed when she fell down four steps at the entrance to her home. Her left ankle was badly fractured and the following morning she had surgery, during which pins were placed to bring four fractured pieces of bone together. The pain was severe.

A mutual friend and I visited with her in the hospital later. Her usual sense of humor presided in spite of her discomfort. She said she had thought about dying, the pros and cons. If she died the pain would stop, but she had a closet full of beautiful clothes that were hardly worn—and now the only place she could wear them was to church.

If she died she would get to see her "ever lovin'" husband, but she'd have to leave her four wonderful sons and her cute grandchildren. Lucy reminded us that her funeral arrangements were in order and said she had called Wally to tell him she might get "carried away" by him in the near future. She was amused at her joke. Wally was not as amused, because he knew that he was about to lose a good friend.

When her sons came to visit her, Lucy had them put her in a wheelchair and take her to the mortuary. She wanted them to approve of her casket selection and review the order of service with her. After making some minor changes in the program since the grandchildren were older, she showed her sons her red dress. They asked her if she wanted to add white doves flying away, fireworks bursting in the air, balloons sailing into the sky, or all of the above. They had inherited her gene for humor, evidently.

While they were there Wally told Lucy's sons about the humorous birthday card she'd sent to him, and about how she'd given him a calendar with beautiful pictures of dogs for Christmas last year. She knew he and his family loved their two Jack Russell terriers. He teased Lucy, saying that he had developed a fondness for these remembrances and that she had to hang around so she could keep sending them. He added that many of his clients never wanted to see him again for some strange reason, and that meant that he needed those who liked him to stay for as long as possible.

Not long after Lucy came home from the hospital, our study group visited her. She stayed on her daybed the whole time, and before we left, she showed us a new lump about the size of a marble on the shinbone of her left leg. It was not painful, but Lucy decided to undergo tests to investigate it.

Two weeks later, my friend called to tell me that the results of Lucy's tests had come back. The verdict was bone cancer and it had spread beyond the leg. The doctors offered her a choice of treatments, but after thinking about it she decided to simply go into hospice and check out. The ankle had been a substantial trial, and she was having problems getting back on that leg. She had done everything in her life that was important to her. Sure, she would love to spend more time with her grandchildren, but she missed her husband more and more. She declared she had had a wonderful life and a great family, and she'd loved her many years of teaching school. It was time to move on.

We went to visit Lucy when she was in hospice at her home. She was free of pain and relaxed as we talked. One of her sons had come with his family to stay. He, too, was a schoolteacher and it was summer vacation, so it was fortunate he had the time to be with his mother. Music came from downstairs. She explained that her grandchildren were practicing a piece for her funeral. The two boys and two girls were accomplished on piano, violin, flute, and cello. She remarked how much she enjoyed listening to them. As we prepared to leave she declared that when she met God, she planned to ask why her husband didn't have to give birth to at least one of their four babies; she said once she got an answer to that, she planned to find her husband, go with him to an isolated cloud, and make joyful sounds.

Two weeks later, Lucy died. We went to the mortuary for the funeral with anticipation, knowing this one would be different. Lucy had been vocal that everyone attending should laugh and have a good time. She set the tone with that gorgeous red dress in the light-colored oak casket.

Wally was there to oversee each of Lucy's requests. The order of service was as she requested. Her oldest son officiated, her youngest gave the eulogy, and her grandchildren played a medley of hymns. They all told stories about growing up with her. Her second son shared a story about the time he and his older brother had gotten into mischief: They were sixteen and fourteen that summer, when they decided to cut up a watermelon, gather fresh peach and pear leftovers from canning, and pick and chop some fresh grapes. Into this mixture they added a couple of cakes of yeast plus sugar from their mother's cupboard, and they threw in some grains of barley just in case. Combining all of this in a ten-gallon bucket with water, they let the mixture sit in the hot dog days of August until the froth on top was well established. Then they slopped the bubbling mixture into the trough for the pigs. Being pigs, the animals noisily smacked it down.

The parents and a farm worker became alarmed when they saw the pigs staggering and falling, rolling in the mud, and making strange sounds. The father didn't need much time to look around for evidence and he smelled some of it in the pig trough. Having had considerable experience raising boys, he asked the necessary questions and got the unnecessary answers. Lucy asked the boys if they were aware they could have killed the pigs. The reply was, "We drank some before we went to bed last night and we're OK today, Mom." Always able to see the humor in life, Lucy laughed at this, despite her disapproval of their prank.

At the conclusion of the service, we were invited to a catered lunch at a nearby church hall where we sat down for a visit with friends and good food plus more reminiscing. Wally joined in. What a way to go!

I remembered a Mark Twain saying, "Let us endeavor to so live that when we die even the undertaker will be sorry." I know there was more than one undertaker sad to see Lucy leave.

~

Thanks to Lucy's foresight and good humor, her family and friends were allowed to experience how death can be so wonderfully included in the process of living. When we embrace the reality of death and personalize our own experience of it, it allows us to transcend pathological anxieties of death that can be so destructive to living our own lives. There is nothing morbid about approaching our own inevitable deaths with this kind of honesty. Lucy's exceptional ability to move past denial helped ease the pain of her passing for her family and friends.

Every funeral gives us an opportunity to view the place of death in our own life. Observing these events reminds each of us in attendance of our own mortal natures. Our feelings and actions are measured and valued.

By talking about her passing, thinking about it, and acting on the reality of death in her future, Lucy provided her sons with coping mechanisms for what the future would assuredly bring. Her attitude was wholesome, not fearful or disturbing, and it was just one of her many gifts to her family.

The Mother Who Couldn't Let Go

My first husband and I were living in the San Fernando Valley in 1959. I had recently given birth to our third baby girl and was taking a maternity leave from the family-owned mortuary where I had worked since I graduated from The Cincinnati School of Mortuary Science in 1945. One night the phone rang it and it was Jim Morrison, a good friend who was also a mortician. He worked for a small competing mortuary located two miles from our home.

"June," he said anxiously, "I have a problem and I need help. I received a call to pick up the body of a six-month-old baby, but the mother won't let go of him. We've tried everything. The doctor was here for an hour, the priest arrived soon after it happened, her husband and her friend have tried every angle, but she just sits there clutching the baby and she won't let anyone come near them."

When I asked how the baby died, he said the baby had a bad cough the day before and started running a high temperature. Eventually the baby seemed to be struggling to breathe, so his parents called in the doctor. Seeing that the baby had stopped breathing completely, the physician performed a tracheotomy as soon as he got to the house, but the baby had already been dead too long for anything to help.

The physician determined that the cause of death was an inflamed epiglottis, a condition that primarily affects children.

The epiglottis is the small lid of cartilage that covers the trachea when we swallow, keeping food from entering our lungs. When it becomes infected it can get inflamed and enlarged, and sometimes it gets lodged in the trachea and prevents breathing. This is what happened to her baby.

"What time did the death occur?" I asked.

"The doctor pronounced him dead at 5:00 p.m."

It was now 9:00 p.m. and my husband was home with my sleeping daughters.

"What do you want me to do?"

"We need to get that baby away from her." He paused, and then said, "Hell, I don't know what to do. If you can't get her to give it to us, the only thing left is brute force. Will you try? Please?"

I dreaded mother/baby scenes, but I also wanted to help. Jim gave me the address and I figured it would take fifteen minutes to drive there. He said the group had gathered in the family room and he would wait at the front entrance for me.

Jim's car was at the curb. I parked behind three cars in the circular driveway. A large magnolia tree shaded the front door from the street light. Jim met me at the bottom of the steps. "She hasn't budged. What ideas do you have?"

I told him to introduce me as a friend, not as a fellow mortician. I also asked that I be left alone with her to talk and that perhaps he could persuade the others to have juice or coffee in the kitchen.

We walked into a spacious, comfortably furnished room. On one wall were many beautifully bound books. The mother rocked to and fro in a platform rocker, cuddling the small form to her breast. Her husband sat on a leather ottoman near her knees. The high-collard priest stood near the fireless fireplace. A woman waited beside him, her arms folded. Jim introduced me to Mrs. Tohill, Mr. Tohill, Father Mority, and a neighbor, Mrs. Clyde. Mr. Tohill pulled a chair with a needlepoint seat alongside the rocker and asked me to sit down. I declined and looked toward Jim. Clearing his throat he said, "Mr. Tohill, could I bother you for some coffee or maybe a drink of water? Perhaps Mrs. Clyde and Father Mority will join us in the kitchen." They heard the earnestness in his voice and left the room.

I sat on the ottoman. Mrs. Tohill continued rocking. At first she ignored me, but then her vacant stare turned to suspicion and then open hostility. With anger she asked, "Who are you?"

I told her my name was June and that I was a friend of Jim's.

"Did you come here to try and take my baby from me?"

"Jim called and asked me to come talk to you, but I'd rather have you talk to me. Do you have other children?" She hesitated, cautiously evaluating any trap she was sure I was setting for her. I continued, "I have three daughters. Is your baby a boy or a girl?"

"He's a boy." Letting her guard down she glanced at the baby. He was dressed only in an undershirt and a diaper. As she moved, I saw a large dried bloodstain on her pale pink blouse. She stroked his fine brown hair that curled softly at the back of his head. "May I see him?" She paused, and then laid the limp body in her lap. The area surrounding his lips was blue. His eyelids, half open, revealed large, clouded, brown eyes. Black blood, caked and cracked, covered the tracheotomy at the base of his throat. Blood saturated the front of his shirt, making it stiff.

"He's a big beautiful baby. Do you have other children?"

"Yes . . ." Muttering, her voice rambled off and I couldn't understand her. Suddenly as if awakening from a sleep, she said, "Yes, Jodie is twelve and Sean is ten. We didn't think we could have any more children; then, he came. His name is Brian. He's such a good baby—so happy. I'd forgotten how much fun a baby can be. He can laugh out loud. Not many babies can do that this early." I touched his outstretched hand. She immediately became defensive and snatched him to her.

"He feels cool. Don't you think you should have a blanket around him?"

Her eyes widened. "You're right. He is cold and he has been so sick. Yes, I need a blanket for him. There's one in the living room on the couch. Will you get it for me?"

"I'd rather hold Brian. I love to hold babies, and I'll be careful with him while you get the blanket. What is your first name?"

"I'm Carol. I'll hurry and get it. Do you think he needs a shawl, too?"

She laid the body in my arms and ran from the room. Returning quickly, she spread the white shawl and placed a receiving blanket on top of it. She was a petite woman with short blonde-streaked hair. Detracting from her beauty, though, were dark, sunken circles under her eyes—eyes that looked so much like little Brian's. She picked up the baby, transferring him to the blanket like she was moving a fragile crystal goblet. Bundling him securely, she eased herself into the rocking hair. The rocker creaked rhythmically back and forth. Her face had a glow about it. "They tried to tell me he's dead, but I know he's not. He is really sick. He just needs some rest and he'll be all right."

"Carol, what time did the doctor tell you he was dead?"
She evaded me. "I'm not sure."
"Were Jodie and Sean home from school?"
She paused. "Yes, they were home. The baby started coughing, then suddenly he couldn't breathe and he turned blue. I called the doctor and it took him an eternity to get here, even if he did say it was only ten minutes. He cut the opening in Brian's throat, but . . ." She looked into space, seeing nothing. "He only needs more rest," she said quietly.

"Was it about five o'clock when Brian stopped breathing?"
"I guess it could have been."
"Where are Jodie and Sean now?"
"They're at Sharon's. She's the woman you met and she lives next door.

"Isn't it time they went to bed? It's ten o'clock."

She studied my face. I thought she was beginning to comprehend that five hours had passed since her baby had shown any sign of life. I waited briefly and then said, "Look, Carol, if you want to sit and rock Brian through the night, I won't try to stop you. No one is going to stop you." Trying to be kind but firm, I continued. "Let's look at what is happening. You are exhausted. I'll wager you got little, if any, sleep last night." Her expression told me I had struck home. "Also, I think that Jodie and Sean are upset. They know something is wrong and they need you. How do you think your husband feels right now? He has not only lost his son, but I'll bet he feels like he's lost you, too." I paused. "Brian needs some attention. He needs a bath and some clean clothes. I am a licensed mortician, and I take care of children who have passed away. I want to take Brian. I'll care for him like he's my own child. It will only take me an hour, then I'll wrap him just as you have and place him in a crib we have at the mortuary. You can see him tomorrow if you like." I stopped to see if she was following me, and then I said, "Carol, will you trust me?"

There was a long minute of silence. She wasn't fighting me. She was fighting tears. "He was so special. God gave him to us when we didn't think there was any hope. I just can't believe this. Why would God take him back? We love him so much." A tear trickled down her cheek.

I persisted, "I'm not going to take him from you. I want you to give him to me. When I leave with him, Father Mority will help you to understand."

Tears welled in her eyes. She whispered, "Ask my husband to come here."

All four of them stood waiting anxiously in the hallway by the family room. I motioned to Mr. Tohil to come in. Father Mority waited with me by the shelves of books. Carol kissed the still, round face, pulled the corner of the shawl down as though to protect him from the cool night air. She handed him to her husband, and then nodded toward me. He walked slowly across the room and placed the baby in my outstretched arms. As I turned to leave, her cries echoed into the hall. I could hear them as I walked down the front steps— long painful sobs.

Jim opened his car door for me. I laid the baby on the seat. "How'd you do it?" he asked.

My larynx hurt as though hands were clasped around it like a vise. Hoping he couldn't hear my sadness, I said softly, "When you become a mother, you won't ask such dumb questions."

⌒

Mrs. Tohill's denial was not uncommon or unwarranted. Shock comes to the survivors, especially when a death is totally unexpected. Shock can be nature's anesthetic, numbing our intense pain. When a loved one is taken from us, it can feel impossible for us to believe it has really happened. It seems impossible and sometimes ethereal. As natural as that response is, at some point (and that point varies greatly) the survivors must deal with reality.

Mrs. Tohill needed help dealing with reality quickly, especially since her husband and children desperately needed her. The fact that we were both mothers was helpful in my assisting her to take her first steps into her grief. Beyond relinquishing the body of her baby, she had a long journey to healing, but she made a substantial step in coping with his death when she handed the small boy to her husband.

While her response to her son's death was extreme, I've experienced many families who've initially refused to accept the reality of death in their lives. An elderly man I helped had long refused to let the doctors remove any life-saving apparatus from his comatose wife because he was convinced she would get better. It wasn't until his children showed him how the skin on her body was slipping off that he was able to let his wife go.

In another instance, a doctor came out of the emergency room where he had tried to resuscitate a man after a heart attack and announced to the man's wife that her husband had passed away and nothing more could be done. She called him a liar, abruptly turned, walked out the door, and drove her car into the country and then to the mountains. Six hours later she returned, confident they would have him in a room and she could talk to him. Her daughter was waiting for her and helped her deal with reality.

When a bereaved person is in shock or denial, they need caring support in facing reality. In all of the cases I've seen, what's been the most effective is when either a clergyperson, a family member, or a close friend can speak patiently but also rationally to the person, gently coaxing them from their denial. Death and tragedy is a reality of life. But together we must face it, in order to heal and continue living our lives.

The Funeral for the Family's Best Friend

In 1961 my husband, an architect, accepted an offer for work he wanted in Salt Lake City, Utah. Soon after we were settled there, I started work in a mortuary that had been in operation for a year.

On a Wednesday evening I stayed to work on an obituary when a woman startled me by appearing suddenly in the doorway to my office. It was late and the doors to the mortuary should have been locked. With black hair falling to her shoulders, wearing a white pantsuit and a green scarf that accented her hazel eyes, she was stunning. I learned later that she owned and operated a modeling school. She looked the part.

"I'm Violet Turner and I need some help. My dog died an hour ago, and I can't bear the thought of having the animal shelter dispose of her. Since there is no animal cemetery in

Salt Lake City, I want to bury her in my back yard."

In response to my asking how I might help, she said, "She was a very special member of our family. I have three children and I dread going home to tell them she is gone. They will be heartbroken."

I related to that. If our family were to lose Tiger, our little brown dachshund, my girls would be devastated. She continued, "I want to plan a brief funeral that they can participate in. That might make it easier for all of us. Lady has been with us for twelve years. My two youngest children do not know what it is like to not have her. Is it possible to have her embalmed, placed in a casket, and laid to rest in a vault?" She hastened to add, "I know it is illegal to bury her in our yard, but if she's in a cement vault with a couple of feet of dirt on top, no one will ever know."

I hesitated to bring a dog into the mortuary, but noting my silence she pressed on persuasively. "We have a large bush in the corner of the yard under which she used to nap. I want her there. I'm willing to pay. Just name your price."

I admired her for wanting to give her children a lesson on death and showing them one way to cope with it. I acquiesced, "I've never done this before, but it's not impossible. I can have a casket made once I see how big she is. The vault is no problem. Do you have someone to dig the grave?"

She didn't, so I promised to talk to the manager at our cemetery. I asked where the dog was. "She's at the vet. Here's a business card. They said they'd wait for you to call."

There were still patients and owners in the veterinarian's waiting room when I arrived. The receptionist dragged a large box from a storage closet and we both carried it out the back door to my car. Once there, I opened the box. Cramped inside was a miniature collie, a small Lassie look-alike, with golden-brown hair, white chest, and white paws.

We had a small preparation room in the garage set up for emergencies. I took the dog there. As I placed her on a table, I surveyed the body and decided I had a major problem. I didn't know how to embalm a dog! I closed her eyes after trimming some eye-caps, and then I tied her mouth loosely with a strip torn from a sheet. Now, where would I find an artery for embalming?

Based on the knowledge that in the human body the femoral artery feeds the legs, I took a guess that dogs might also have a major artery in their groin. Rolling her onto her back, I felt the softness of the white hair spread thinly over her belly. Making a small incision, I was lucky to find two vessels fairly near the skin, though I questioned whether either of them was thick enough to be an artery.

When morticians embalm bodies, we must rely on our sense of touch as well as sight to help guide us in achieving the proper distribution of fluid and recognizing when we have injected enough. We touch the arms, legs, trunk walls, eyelids, and lips to determine the correct degree of firmness. But with this dog, I couldn't feel or see through all of her fur. I realized that the only gauge I had was her nose. I felt it. It was soft.

After injecting for a couple of minutes her nose was firm to my touch, so I tied the vessels and sutured the small incision. I then posed her like she was asleep in front of a fireplace with her front paws outstretched and her head resting on them, tucking her hind legs up under her body. After shampooing and drying her with a hairdryer, I moved her to a transfer table. She was beautiful and I was proud of her.

The white casket measuring three feet in length was delivered the next afternoon, and a groundsman from the cemetery agreed to dig the grave. I called Violet; we decided to hold the graveside service the next morning at 10:00 a.m.

I delivered the casket with the dog to the family home in a white van and backed into their driveway. I saw no need to alarm a neighborhood with a funeral coach. Violet, her two preteen daughters, and her nine-year-old son Timothy carried the casket to the grave and sat it on the supports. Then Violet started the ceremony.

"We'll all miss you, Lady," she began. "You weren't just a watch dog, you were also the best baby sitter I ever had. We gave you a couch all your own, but through all these years you thought you were fooling me. I knew that after I went to bed at night, you climbed the stairs quietly and slept on Tim's bed. I heard you get up before me every morning and creep down the stairs and climb on your couch, pretending to sleep when I came down. Our home will be empty without you." Violet wiped her eyes and stroked Lady.

The girls were crying. Tim spoke, "She was no dog. She

was my best friend. She understood everything I said to her. Whenever I had any trouble, I would tell her all about it and she'd sit with her head on my knees until I finished, then she'd lick my face and I knew she understood. I don't know what I'll do without her." His voice broke and his mother hugged him. She nodded to me. I closed the lid and helped the groundsman lower the small casket down into the cement vault at the bottom of the grave. Placing one strap through a hook on the vault lid, we slowly lowered it to its place. All of us left when the man reached for his shovel.

Two weeks later, I delivered a small gray granite marker to be set in the corner under her bush. The inscription read, "You'll Always Be Our Lady."

———

In the thirty years I directed funerals, it was not unusual to have children attending services conducted in traditional churches. Occasionally, the family would arrange to have a nursery in the building where children who created any disturbance could be taken. Most of the children were well behaved, and they seemed to have been prepared for the event.

My own children were introduced to death as babies when they went to work with me on occasion. It was simply a part of their lives. Without my prompting, they chose their own caskets by the age of ten. During family gatherings, the children were known to play hide-and-seek among the caskets (my nieces and nephews still tell me those are some of their favorite memories growing up). This close proximity to death did not mitigate my children's degree of loss when a friend, grandparent, or stepfather passed away, but they were spared the shocking pain that comes with denying that death is a part of life.

In 1972, my manager gave to me a book titled *The Many Faces of Grief,* by Edgar N. Jackson, who is a minister and a PhD in clinical psychology. He was a pioneer in understanding grief. In this book is a chapter titled "Children and Grief." The following paragraph concludes and summarizes that chapter:

"There are some things we should always keep in mind when dealing with children. First, we should try to understand where they are in terms of their emotional development. This is basic for meaningful communication. Second, we should realize that it may be possible to confuse children by misinformation, but that children have built-in lie detectors and can sense when they are being deceived. They will quickly lose confidence in those dishonest persons to whom they must nevertheless turn for guidance and understanding. Also, it is important to realize that children want to participate in family ceremonies and are never too young to share in a funeral designed to show the value of life. But should a child not want to participate in a funeral, it is a danger signal; for it shows that the child has already picked up anxiety about death, and this will be an important concern in working through the child's apprehension about the rites that accompany death."

By having a funeral for Lady, Violet introduced her children to the reality of death as part of life. She also taught them the value of gathering together to support each other in a funeral service. These children were left better prepared to handle the inevitable occasions later in their lives when they would encounter the death of a family member or friend. Violet also modeled how to behave at a funeral by speaking first so the children could follow her example of what to say when celebrating a life. The more we know about death, the less we fear it. And when fear isn't blocking us, we're better prepared to deal with whatever life (and death) sends our way.

Departing Thoughts

I took the a casket with the body of an eighty-four-year-old man to the chapel in The Little Sisters of the Poor, an assisted-living care facility under the auspices of the Catholic Church in East Los Angeles. There the resident priest led a group of fifty residents in the rosary and conducted a Mass. At the conclusion, I opened the casket and invited those who cared to view to step forward. Most of those attending passed by the casket before leaving, and soon the group dwindled down to three women visiting nearby.

Two of the women left, and the one remaining woman stepped to the casket aided by a cane. She was a bright woman, with her white hair freshly curled. She looked at the deceased for a full minute, made the sign of the cross, and turned to me. "He was such a nice man with gentle ways and a soft voice. Everyone liked him. He was a great bridge player, too." She smiled and said she was ninety-four years old and had lived at this facility for the past eighteen years. The friends she made there were "good people."

Then she turned, laid her hand on his folded hands, and said wistfully, "It's too bad he had to die so young."

Chapter Two

Embracing Grief

Mortician's Diary

It was a critical time in my life when I graduated from The Cincinnati College of Mortuary Science in 1945 and started seeking an apprenticeship. There were few licensed women in the business. As the only woman in my class of '45, I constituted 5 percent of our group (by the 1995 class, 35 percent of the students were young women). After three months and seventy-nine letters to mortuaries in four western states, along with seventy-nine rejections, my oldest sister, Beth, helped me find work in a family-owned mortuary located in Hollywood, California.

On my first Sunday in Hollywood, I went to church. There I met Erma, a thin girl with delicate features and a mild overbite. After an afternoon of good food and conversation, I learned that Erma was looking for a roommate; I was looking for a place to live.

Living together was a learning experience for both of us. We were on opposite sides of the fence politically. She was athletically inclined; I loved to read and write. She worked at Farmer's Insurance Agency as a file clerk and she stammered.

Like most people who stammer, she never hesitated on words when she sang, swore, or expressed anger. When she told a joke I had to exercise patience as she told the punch line.

As we reviewed our schedules together, she said she would be late coming home on Thursday evenings because she had a weekly appointment with a psychiatrist. She explained she was seeking a solution to her stammering. The therapist back home in Utah believed she had a physical speech impediment, but her own experience convinced her the problem was an emotional one. She'd moved to Los Angeles to see a doctor who was highly recommended in this field.

I asked, "What do the two of you talk about?"

She replied, "I t-t-tell him a l-l-lot of s-stuff I w-want to believe, and h-he t-t-ells me s-ssstuff I refuse to b-b-believe." I never broached the subject again.

We went grocery shopping one Saturday in the hot days of August. Each of us carried two bags of groceries; as we neared the top of the thirty-six stairs leading up the hill to our apartment, Erma fell headfirst to the ground. I turned her over to see if she was conscious. Her face was alarmingly pale; her pulse was rapid and thready. As I started to call for an ambulance, she stirred and weakly motioned "No" with her hand. It took a minute for her to gather strength. Then she said, "D-d-don't g-get excited, just l-l-let m-m-me lie still f-for a m-m-minute." Resting later on our couch, she explained she had a heart murmur that gave her trouble occasionally. It was no big deal and I should forget it.

On a warm night in July three years later, Erma and I were lying in bed chatting before going to sleep. We breathed in deeply, enjoying the fragrance from the night-blooming jasmine tree that grew near our open window (Erma called it "the bloomin' night jasmine"). Erma announced her plans to return to Utah for college and take the necessary year to complete her degree in elementary education. She wasn't sure what she wanted to do with the rest of her life, but she hoped to find her answer in school. I enjoyed Erma and I hated to see her leave, but I recognized there was no appreciable difference in her speech in spite of the hours and money she had spent in therapy. For her sake, I thought she needed a different approach to the problem, and I hoped school might hold it. Before going to sleep she murmured, "I'll m-miss that t-t-tree. It smells l-like someone r-r-ran over the Avon l-l-ady."

Over the twenty years that followed that night, Erma and I spent time together as our lives allowed. When I married, there was a telegram from Erma waiting at the Dude Ranch where my husband and I honeymooned: "I wish you a lifetime of happiness and companionship. I also wish I was there to put honey on your john. Oceans of love, Erma."

Wherever Erma turned she faced discrimination because of her speech impediment. She wanted to have a teaching role at her church, but even in an elected position she was relegated to other, less-important tasks because a leader feared that her impediment might keep some people from attending when she conducted. When she applied for a counseling job at a high school, she was placed in "an important position in the administrative office."

But Erma persevered, and finally in 1958 she found a personnel director in the Los Angeles Unified School District who placed his confidence in her and hired her to teach third-grade students in Norwalk, where she developed a reading and spelling program that was so successful it was incorporated into the entire school district. From there, in 1962, she went to teach kindergarten children among the Navajo. It was the first program of its kind, and in that position she was on the faculty of the University of Utah. She told me she did not stammer at all around the students or their mothers. She said, "They are s-s-so accepting."

In March of 1965, she called. "Where are you?" I asked.

"I'm r-relaxing in the M-M-Memorial Hospital"

"I can see *you* relaxing. What's the trouble?"

When she told me she would be there for a few days, I went to visit. I located her on the third-floor surgery wing. Sitting up in bed, she looked out the window toward the beautiful Mt. Olympus of the Wasatch Range. When I saw some color in her cheeks, I told her how much better she looked in the hospital than out of it. She laughed.

She confided she had been in the same hospital two years earlier for a heart catheterization. The doctors found the arteries leading from the heart to the upper portion of her body to be small. This accounted for the blackouts she had had all of her life. The procedure had helped, but now she was relapsing and the doctors thought she shouldn't be driving for fear she might pass out at the wheel. She couldn't continue her work on the reservation without a car.

She had agreed to a second procedure, although the medical team told her she stood a 50/50 chance of survival if it was successful. Her chances without it were nil.

She asked me many questions about mortuaries and the costs her father would shoulder. When I started to get upset, she laughed me off by saying she favored her 50 percent chance of walking out of the hospital.

Since she was scheduled for surgery on Monday, I visited her on Sunday evening.

Erma was sitting cross-legged on the bed reading a book in which she was so engrossed she didn't hear me enter. When she laid the book down, I picked it up, *Lady Chatterley's Lover*. I've heard of this."

"There's nothing wrong with it. My brother the English professor has made it required reading for his students."

"I've heard that if they cut out the sex scenes all they'd have left is a leaflet."

"So what? If I can't have the real thing, I'll get it vicariously." We both laughed and I noticed how pretty she was. Her eyes sparkled and her cheeks were pink. When I could see her tiring, I left. As I reached for the elevator down button, I realized it was my first conversation with her when she had not stammered even once.

On Tuesday morning, Erma's father called me. With sadness

he told me that as Erma stood by her bed about 6:00 a.m., intending to wash her face, she had collapsed on the floor and the doctors were unable to resuscitate her. He wanted me to care for her.

Since I was so emotionally involved, I knew I couldn't embalm the body. I asked my ski-tanned co-embalmer, Russ, to stay and embalm. Erma had agreed to an invasive autopsy in the hopes that doctors could learn something from her abnormality that could help others. It was difficult for me emotionally to see what had been done to her body, but as I bathed her remains, I noticed she had shaved her legs and underarms. Her toenails and fingernails were manicured with a new coat of bright-red polish. True to herself, Erma had again been attentive to every detail. She knew that details constituted the whole of life, and she always paid minute attention to details in her relationships with friends and family. She knew many people because in 1955 she traveled by herself around the world, making friends all the way. Always ready for another adventure, Erma had been prepared for life or death when she entered the hospital.

Erma's family of four brothers and four sisters gathered at the family home. We took the casket there, where Erma's body stayed overnight before being transported to the local church the next morning. The church was filled to capacity for her funeral. A Native American mother with a papoose strapped into a cradleboard passed me on her way to the church. Two nuns in black habits waited by the door. Three olive-skinned women wearing saris sat in the chapel. Six of Erma's nephews had been named as pallbearers.

The first speaker, one of Erma's college professors, told the congregation that there were students in his classes who had higher IQs but none had worked harder than she had. A church leader praised her devotion to her faith and her family, her years of dedicated work with Girl Scouts, and her courageous travels around the world making many friends.

Following the service, the funeral procession made its way to a small country cemetery with tall evergreens and erect tombstones. Afterward, I declined the family's invitation to join them for lunch at the house. I needed to go home and embrace my own grief.

Once home, all I felt was anger. I was angry with the doctors who had performed the autopsy and taken apart the body that had served her so well. I was angry with God for not "taking care" of Erma. Her death seemed grossly unfair. She spent forty years trying to solve the problem with her speech impediment. On the Sunday before she died, I heard with my own ears the ease with which she spoke. I witnessed that she had finally conquered this lifelong frustration. Two days later her life, with her victory, was gone. I remembered a professor of philosophy who stated in one of my classes, "There is no such thing as fair." I wondered why there was so much *un*fairness in a world where there was no fair?

It was nearly a year before I could accept that God *had* "taken care" of Erma—just not how I had wanted. My anger slowly dissipated with each grieving family I assisted and each loved one I helped lay to rest. Every time I went to work I was reminded that we will all die sometime—and that most often that time feels too soon to the people who survive us. In this way, death is neither fair nor unfair; it just is. And no amount of resistance on my part could change that.

Even in the height of my grief and anger, I knew that I would eventually find resolution if I was patient with myself. It took time for me to realize that I was stuck in anger because I couldn't stop thinking about Erma's struggle for all those years to overcome her speech disability. It just seemed so unfair that she wasn't able to better enjoy her last-minute progress. Then one day, after observing my own daughter struggling with the symptoms of her cerebral palsy, I had to accept the fact that trials are just a part of life. Erma was no exception. And, in some way, the trials she faced made her the wisecracking, lighthearted, and deeply compassionate person that she was.

Over time, I was able to focus more of my energy remembering the life Erma had led, rather than on the timing and circumstance of her death. I missed Erma's humor and her wise mind. I will always remember her affection and caring for everyone she knew. I can even understand her politics. And, luckily for me, she will be a part of my life for as long as I live.

The Mother Who Risked Her Life to Grieve

While driving to work in downtown Los Angeles, I heard a news bulletin on the radio that another murder had occurred in South Central Los Angeles. Police were saying it looked like a gang killing. In 1992 South Central was a hotbed of racial strife. For years, it had been occupied almost solely by African Americans, but now many Hispanics were moving in and things were crowded, tense, and often violent. I noted the name of the victim, Ernesto Diaz, and I hoped the family didn't choose our mortuary for reasons that will soon become clear.

Around noon I received a telephone call from a Mormon bishop. He made an appointment for 3:00 p.m. to bring in the mother of a seventeen-year-old boy who had been killed yesterday. The boy's name was Ernesto Diaz.

Later that day Bishop Rodriguez introduced me to Mary Diaz, a pretty woman with dark circles under her eyes. I judged her to be in her mid-thirties. She told me that Ernesto was her only child. With a hint of defiance, she said, "My son was not a gang member." She told me he had been standing near their apartment-house entrance with some friends when three shots were fired from a passing car. One bullet struck Ernesto in his head, killing him instantly.

Bishop Rodriguez agreed with Mary saying, "I can't believe he ever affiliated with a gang. He joined our church two years ago and he has attended all of his meetings, showing up every Sunday in a white shirt and tie."

Mary interrupted, "He always attended church with me until three years ago when he went around with some kids that were sort of wild. When he made friends with some Mormons and wanted to join their church, it was OK with me."

When I started asking for vital statistical information for the death certificate, Mary handed a copy of Ernesto's birth certificate to me. It stated her name as the mother, and the father's name was listed "unknown." I thought she didn't want to answer that question verbally in front of the bishop.

Bishop Rodriguez, a short man with streaks of gray in his black hair, told me Mary had little money so his church would be paying for a modest church service. Because Mary was a practicing Catholic, he'd spoken with her parish priest who said that with his recommendation the Catholic cemetery in South Los Angeles would donate the burial, including a grave.

Bishop Rodriguez, believing that funerals were for the living, agreed on behalf of his church to pay for a Catholic service. Mary said her priest would have a recitation of the rosary in our chapel on Friday night and a Mass would be celebrated on Saturday morning in the church. The bishop would offer a prayer at the graveside as his part of the ceremonies. I verified the times and submitted the obituary to the *Los Angeles Times*.

Friday night arrived, and our chapel began to fill with young people, some dressed in their Sunday best, and others dressed in sagging pants and backwards baseball caps. One boy had a red bandana tied snugly around his head.

Three women accompanied Mary to her seat so the service could begin. The priest donned his vestments, I handed him a vial of holy water, and he entered the chapel.

Suddenly, a car outside revved its engine and we heard the squealing of tires. That's when the bullets started to fly.

I heard gunshots, and then the tinkling of shattered glass as bullets rained through the stained-glass windows. Everyone hit the floor, including the priest and me.

I was at the entrance with no way to exit except to go outside. Bullets lodged in the double doors next to me, open to the entrance from the street. I saw the priest on his hands and knees rapidly crawling to the nearby receptionist and phone. The rest of us stayed down. In a couple of minutes we heard sirens and soon the footsteps of the police on the roof of the chapel, where they could oversee two streets.

The priest hastily concluded and announced that Mass the next morning was going to be private for family members only. He admonished the audience to leave carefully. The young people were orderly and quiet as they left. A police officer stood by the exit. I went immediately to Mary, who was pale and trembling.

The priest came to her and said he thought having a congregation at the church the next morning would be an open invitation for another attack. He felt the Mass was necessary, but we needed to limit the number of cars traveling to the cemetery. A police officer joined our small group. He said that two police cars would escort us to the cemetery in the morning because none of us had any idea who had fired on us that night and who might pursue the group tomorrow. He said one patrol car would escort the group in front of the hearse and one would follow. I volunteered to pick Mary up on Saturday morning and remain with her throughout the day. The priest and the bishop agreed to ride together so we would only have three cars to be escorted.

I walked with Mary and her friends to their car. They were all shocked at what had happened, but one of the women said she was going to stay with Mary that night.

The events went smoothly on Saturday with no further problems.

At the conclusion of the graveside service, while the priest talked with Mary, I walked to the two policemen waiting for us to leave. They told me this death had all the markings of being gang related. It need not mean Ernesto was a gang member. A mistaken identity was always possible. He might have belonged to a gang at one time, however briefly. He might have considered joining and vocalized his intent, then not followed through. He might have offended a gang member—even innocently or without realizing it. They also questioned what might have been in Mary's past. There were many possible explanations for this tragedy.

Traveling home, Mary was quiet—too quiet. I tried for conversation but she answered briefly. Then unexpectedly she said, "I feel like I owe you an explanation of why I don't know who the father of my child is. When I was sixteen years old, I was gang raped. I went to a party and drank too much and passed out. I only have the word of two friends about what happened, but I was told four teenaged boys were involved. I didn't tell my parents until I was about six months along and it was becoming obvious. It was also too late to do much more than just have the baby because I hardly knew anything about those who were at the party. I was pretty stupid." She looked at me to see how I reacted.

I asked, "When did you come to Los Angeles?"

"Well, we lived in Chicago and Mom helped with the baby and I worked. Later I came out here with my son, to try to get away from the past. I've been so afraid ever since that night at the party that someone else is going to try and hurt me. I found it easy to get lost in Los Angeles, but it has been lonely here. I guess it will be a lot lonelier now."

We were nearing her home and I asked, "What are you going to do now that you are alone?"

"I have the week off from work, and I'm planning to spend the whole time just letting myself cry. I haven't been able to cry because I've been so afraid. I can't believe someone killed my son right outside our own home. But I can't hold it in anymore. There's always something to be afraid of, but now that my worst fears have already come true, I can't hide anymore."

As tragic and terrifying as this funeral was, I still remember it with some appreciation. In particular, it was refreshing to see the way the two churches came together with fairness, compassion, and respect for each other and for the mother. It was also heartening to see them support this woman who was so in need, and to see how grateful and thankful she was for their help. At one point she said she had fifty-five dollars in her purse and she offered to pay on the charges, but the bishop told her she would need that for herself. Both clergy seemed knowledgeable of her circumstances and acted in good faith of her needs. She seemed to be very much alone. I was glad the clergy came through for her.

All of Mary's life seemed to be centered round her son. I'm sure her dreams were too. With his life gone, she faced a Herculean task carrying on without him. Mary had all of her fear stuffed inside her. I think it influenced her inability to cry until the details concerning the death were all cared for. But she was also wise because she knew she had to grieve and she set aside the time when she could do it unencumbered by the numerous other problems she faced. I admired her not only for her wisdom but for knowing herself as she did.

The Widow Who Needed a Way to Say Goodbye

Janice Bott had beautiful white hair pulled back from her angular face. Andrew, her husband, had just died after open-heart surgery at the age of seventy-six. They both had prearranged services with our mortuary, and in their plan it stated he was to be cremated and scattered over the Pacific Ocean. He specified "No funeral service." Janice wistfully said she could afford the best funeral service for him, but she wouldn't go against his wishes.

After she signed our form to authorize his cremation, she started to tell me about their marriage. They had met in college and married a year later. Andrew went back to school to get his Masters Degree in business administration and graduated with honors. He first managed the budget of a large hospital in Los Angeles, then he controlled all business at a university in the Midwest, and finally he ended his career with a twenty-five-year stint as a West Coast executive with Blue Cross.

They decided when they married that they wouldn't have children because they both wanted to travel extensively. She was a travel agent with years of experience and she never wanted for a position. Her job required her to travel, and his positions always allowed him to schedule the time off when they wanted to go together. They had been all over the world and loved it. They carried pictures of the most memorable places they had seen.

However, as they aged and Andrew's health became problematic, they were not able to keep the pace they once had. They missed having the children and grandchildren all of their friends bragged about. The Botts owned two dogs named Barney and Fluffy and loved them as family but still felt the loss of not having children. Janice started to cry when she said, "With Andrew gone I'm so lonely I could die. If I had it to do over again—I'd have twelve kids." I sympathized with her pain and with her regrets about the path not chosen, though I knew from professional experience that even widows with children know intense loneliness when they lose their mate.

Two months later Janice called for an appointment. After I brought her a cup of coffee in my office, she told me about trying to go on a cruise. When she reached the first port, she flew home. It was no use. She was miserable. She went to New Jersey to visit the only relative she had—a cousin she hadn't seen in years. She lasted two days and was such poor company she thought she should leave. Her mind refused to function as it had; she seemed to be in mental rut. All she could think about was Andrew. She cried as she said, "Maybe Andrew didn't need a funeral service, but I do."

Since she was a practicing Catholic, she met with a priest and they planned a Mass for the following week, which was to be followed by a catered lunch. I placed newspaper notices for her in the obituary columns of local papers. She wanted to mail announcements to their friends and his associates at

Blue Cross. Janice worked with a caterer to select a menu for a buffet luncheon. I ordered the prayer cards she selected and prepared a register for guests to sign. She asked me to come to the church and direct her guests. I planned to go early to arrange placement of the floral pieces she wanted me to order. For that week, Janice put all of her efforts into planning a lovely send-off for Andrew.

Everything went as planned. The church had arranged for an organist and soloist. More than one hundred guests attended and stayed for lunch. The hall was lovely, with pastel cloths on the tables and centerpieces of fresh flowers. People talked, laughed, and simply enjoyed the hour together with food and drink. At the end of the afternoon, I presented Janice with the remainder of the prayer cards, the signed register, and copies of the obituary notices.

Later, I received a letter from Janice thanking me for helping her. Since the funeral she'd started to feel much better. She'd begun serving as a volunteer at an elementary school tutoring children who were having trouble learning to read, something she had always wanted to do. There were two trips she had in mind, but she said she wasn't going to make any definite plans until she was more comfortable in her life as a single person. From what I've seen in my life and in my work, it's my guess that she eventually took those trips and enjoyed them. Because over time, most of us learn to reconnect with the pleasures that life can offer us while we're still around to enjoy them.

～

It seems to be a growing trend to turn away from the traditional funeral service, sometimes replacing it with a gathering on a golf course, or a beach, or even a bar, and other times abandoning a ceremony completely. From my perspective, this is a great loss to society and to those in mourning. A funeral is a pause in our life to acknowledge that a life has been lived. It allows mourners to remember and honor that life in a special way. It is a chance for family and friends to gather and give emotional and physical support to one another. It provides closure for some. It brings to all of our minds the reality and finality of death. We use the funeral as an opportunity to express our thoughts and feelings to the surviving family members and loved ones, helping them to better cope with their grief and move forward with their lives.

Maybe not everyone benefits from a funeral service, but many people need one more than they realize. Janice Bott did. She was healthier for recognizing her need to commemorate her husband's life and acting on that need. Funerals are for the living, not the dead. They help us embrace our grief by moving us along in the grieving process. They make our losses, as well as our joys, somehow more real. After the funeral, Janice was able to see that she needed activities to steer her thoughts into new directions. From there she could build a new life for herself.

The Orphan Who Came to the Funeral

She seemed little more than a child as she sat in an uphol-stered chair in front of my desk. Her hair was cut short with bangs that blended into soft brown curls surrounding her face. Her name was Cindy Conrad and her mother's body lay in our preparation room.

She told me she was an only child. Her father died three years ago and was buried in our cemetery. There was a grave next to him for her mother. When I indicated I would first take the information we needed for the death certificate, she responded firmly, "No, first I want to talk about prices."

"Our prices depend on what you want us to do. Do you want a chapel or a graveside service? Do you want ground burial or cremation?"

"Give me all the alternatives and the prices and then I'll tell you," she said.

Taking a pad of paper I made five columns titling them: 1. Chapel service and ground burial. 2. Graveside service and burial. 3. Direct burial with no services. 4. Cremation and burial of cremains in grave, and 5. Cremation and scatter at sea. Then I listed what would be required in each option and the total cost. The most expensive cost $4,460. The least was No. 5 totaling $350.

Biting her pencil, she said, "I can't scatter her at sea. She wanted to be near Dad."

Studying the figures silently for a few moments, she pointed to No. 4. "I can raise enough money to cremate her and bury the ashes in her grave next to Dad. I can't possibly afford a casket or a funeral."

Proceeding with my paperwork, I commented, "You are pretty young to be going through this."

"I'm twenty-five going on fifty," she said wearily with a faint smile.

"What caused your mother's death?"

"Cancer. She's been fighting it for three years, but it spread all over her body. She didn't stand a chance."

"I see that she died at home. Have you had help in caring for her?"

She told me that six months prior her mother had been so weakened by chemotherapy that Cindy had put her into a nursing home because she worried about leaving her mother alone all day. They lived on her wages and a small pension from her father. After a week her mother couldn't stand it. She pleaded to be brought home, promising she would do everything in her power to take care of herself. Cindy said, "I didn't have the heart to make her stay there. I could handle the cooking and cleaning at home. She took her own bath and watched the clock to take her medications. I fixed her breakfast and left her lunch by her bed."

She went on to tell me that last night when she came home she looked into her mother's room. Her mom was lying on her side with her back to the door evidently sleeping.

Cindy turned on the television and watched a program before she realized her mother usually snores and no sound was coming from the bedroom. She hurried to check on her mother and found her dead.

I said to Cindy, "You're pretty cool and collected after what you've been through."

She shrugged her shoulders. "Mom's death is only the end of the beginning. It all began ten years ago when my father had a stroke. For seven years he sat in his wheelchair and the only words he ever spoke—and he said them every day all day—were 'I'm goin' back to work tomorrow.' We heard those words millions of times! His death was a big relief for all of us."

She continued, telling me that three months after her father's death, her mother learned she had cancer of the lungs although she had never smoked. It was inoperable so they got what mileage they could from chemotherapy. As Cindy studied her hands intently, she suddenly said she had to go get the money from her boss. She was a legal secretary and promised to bring the money tomorrow.

I was concerned about her going home to an empty house. "What will you do this evening?"

"I'm going home, take a couple of good stiff drinks, and forget the last ten years ever happened."

"Today is Tuesday. The cremation will take place tomorrow, and on Thursday I'll have the cremains interred in her grave. Do you want to go to the grave with me at 11:00 a.m. and witness the interment?"

"Why?" I wasn't sure if she asked this innocently or if she was challenging me to give her a good reason to attend.

My feelings toward her at that moment were maternal. I put my arm around her shoulder, gave her a hug, and said, "My thinking is that maybe if you participate in paying final tribute to your mother as we lay her remains to rest, it will bring you more peace of mind than the hangover you have planned for yourself. But you think about it and let me know if you want to go with me."

As the service time approached on Thursday, I had the urn in my arms and was ready to leave the office when a call came from Cindy. She said her car was stalled and asked if I would wait for her. It was forty-five minutes before she came with two neighbors. She had gone to one neighbor to bring her but that woman's car had a flat tire. They went to a second neighbor who brought them. Cindy carried a bouquet of pink asters wrapped in green tissue paper.

I handed the urn to the groundskeeper, who placed it in a vault and proceeded to fill in the small grave. After he tamped the final piece of sod in place, Cindy sat down on the ground by the fresh grave and arranged the asters so they covered the small spot.

Glancing up at me, she said, "I was wallowing in self-pity when I met with you on Tuesday and I'm sorry. I went home and thought. I thought about the fact that I was born with congenital hip problems. I wore casts on both legs until I was nearly three. Mom had to lift and carry me all the time. She saw how lonely I was, so she made the lemonade pinker and painted funny faces on cookies with frosting just to coax the kids inside to play with me. Those were the days when Barbie dolls were new and she made some of the most gorgeous Barbie clothing you've ever seen. Dad made every piece of doll furniture imaginable. I was the envy of every kid in our neighborhood."

She continued, "Then when Dad had his stroke, she refused to put him in a nursing home. She changed his diapers and exercised his arms and legs. She bathed and fed him for those long seven years. If I can be just half the lady she was, I'll be great."

She kissed the ends of her fingers and pressed them gently into the grass that covered the cremains. "Goodbye, Mom, I love you!"

Rising to her feet, she said, "Thanks for encouraging me to come today. Instead of forgetting it all happened, I feel good remembering some wonderful times, too." She picked up two blossoms and laid them tenderly on her father's grave. The four of us walked under a bright sun back to our cars to say goodbye.

Cindy was grieving for her parents for ten years before they were both gone. The illnesses of both parents would be tragic for anyone. She'd begun this journey when she was only fifteen years old. She said they were relieved when her father died, and after her mother's three years of a fatal illness, she probably felt some relief again. It's a natural response after such a prolonged period of suffering. Research has shown that moving through the experience of an illness with a loved one often reduces the acuteness of grief when the death occurs. Anticipating the event makes it easier to go forward as we plan for the event and consider how we will move on afterward. That didn't mean Cindy's grief was over; her life would be different without her parents, and she would likely feel the pain of that, especially when she couldn't share the monumental events of her life with them. Still, I think that being there when her mother was laid to rest was a positive force in Cindy's ability to move forward with her life.

Cindy didn't think of the small gathering at the grave as a funeral, but it was. There was a beautiful eulogy and a tribute to a loving mother. Funerals, no matter how big or small, create an atmosphere for the expression of deep feelings and the reaching out for support. Our numbers were few that day, but our support and sympathy were there for this young woman who had seen almost overwhelming trials.

Departing Thoughts

Donna, a petite woman wearing her blonde hair in a pageboy, came to the mortuary with her sister to make arrangements for the cremation of the body of her husband. Her sister immediately asked me to bring a glass of water, saying Donna might need more medicine. She held a prescription bottle in her hand.

I asked the routine questions for information we would need on the death certificate, such as her husband's birthplace, birthdate, Social Security number, and parent's full names. With heavy eyelids, Donna responded hesitantly and she needed to amend some of her responses. I learned that her husband was a forty-three-year-old physician who had previously told her his heart had a tendency to speed up occasionally but it was nothing to worry about. She completely forgot about it until she awakened in the night and found his body lifeless. This event was definitely not in their plans, and she sat for an unknown amount of time in shock.

She told me, "As the numbness faded, I was angry. I reached over and punched him on the arm. I told him dying on me was one thing. Leaving me with three teenage boys to raise was something else!" The fury in her voice suggested her rage had not yet subsided. The sister insisted she take another pill to "help her calm down." While not overly common, this wasn't the first time I'd seen someone overmedicate a bereaved loved one to try to contain or banish their painful feelings. It's always been my feeling that a funeral is a time to grieve fully and forcibly; while every case is different and some medications may sometimes be warranted, going through a funeral so drugged that you can't remember it doesn't help anyone in the long run. These medications can prolong the immediate reactions (such as anger) and delay the beginning of a healthy grieving process. Again it is the age-old question: How much is too little or when is it too much?

When I asked Donna what she wanted us to do with her husband's cremated remains, she told me to scatter his ashes in the mountains. Anywhere, she said. She did not particularly care. He loved to camp out and fish, especially with his boys, so it seemed an appropriate disposition at that time.

Some months later Donna called me to ask if I had scattered the cremains yet. I told her I hadn't had an occasion to go to the mountains, so I was still holding them. I assured her I would do it by spring.

A month before Memorial Day, Donna appeared in the mortuary and again asked if I had taken the cremains to the mountains. I replied, "No, I haven't. I've been waiting for you to come in and change your mind. It's just a hunch I have had."

She looked at me, surprised, and began to cry. For the first time she didn't seem sedated, and her emotional response felt genuine and warranted. "I am so relieved," she explained. "My boys want a place to go put flowers, a place where they can think about their dad. They have missed him so much, and I was thinking more about me when I came in to make arrangements. I haven't known what to do."

I gave her some options, including a space in a cremains garden, but she chose to purchase a full-sized grave that could accommodate additional urns or even a casket.

She authorized the cemetery to inter the cremains in the grave and place a bronze marker on it with the salutation, "Beloved Husband, Father, and Physician," followed by his name and dates of his birth and death.

I ordered the engraving and promised her everything would be in place for Memorial Day. I was out in the cemetery that day helping visitors locate graves, and I noticed Donna with her three sons sitting on their spot around a red rose wreath they had placed. They stayed for an hour.

Occasionally after that day, I would see one or more of the family visiting there. The oldest boy seemed to come more than the others. He often brought a book and would sit and read. I also noted Donna visiting the grave alone occasionally. Whenever I saw them, I thought about how glad I was that we hadn't scattered the ashes before Donna could make a choice that better suited her sons' needs.

Chapter Three

Overcoming Tragedy

Mortician's Diary

Our farm was in the Upper Snake River Valley in southeastern Idaho. The large window in our living room framed the three peaks of the mighty Teton Mountains. I was the fifth of six children, three boys and three girls.

The Depression set upon us suddenly. The moment is still vivid in my mind. I was five years old. My father came out of the bank in our small town and got into the car where my older sister and I waited. "All of our money is gone," he said. I felt no apprehension at the news. We raised our food on the farm. My mother sewed all my clothes. It occurred to me that several thousand of Dad's sheep might go hungry, but I knew he would provide for us. He always had.

Money was short and it became even more so when Dad had to sell the sheep to pay debts. We had recently brought running water into our home. We even had heated water from a tank near the coal stove. Pumping water and hauling in coal and kindling every day were tasks we'd grown up with, and now we were suddenly relieved of those responsibilities. After using the inside bathroom for a few days, I decided that life could hardly be much better. In this way I learned that even though life sends us difficulties, it also sends small comforts to help us along the way.

Tragic life events also change who we are and how we live our lives—sometimes for the worse, but often also for the better. I was barely fourteen years old when my mother became very ill. She spent ten days in the hospital in Idaho Falls where the doctors performed all the tests they knew and could not find a cause. They diagnosed her with a severe nervous breakdown. Upon returning home she was bedridden and rarely spoke. She was mired in a deep sadness of a kind I had never seen. My sister Beth, a registered nurse, came home for a week and taught me how to give a bed bath and change my mother while she was in bed. I devised a way to wash my mother's black hair using oilcloth and a bucket. Her hair fell below her waist when she stood. I loved to brush it. My father, my brother Rex, and I cared for Mother for two years during her illness. She began getting stronger during the second year but her recovery was gradual. Those two years I spent caring for her were intensely painful at times, but ultimately they had wonderful lessons for me. They instilled in me an ability to care for those in emotional pain, something that served me well in my line of work. They taught me patience and acceptance, which I keenly needed when, years later, I gave birth to a severely disabled daughter. They helped give me the strength that I drew upon not long ago, when I became a caretaker for my terminally ill second husband, Ed. And they gave me a reference point when, some twenty years after my mother fell ill, I was hospitalized with the same symptoms. By that time the ailment had a name: clinical depression. Only then did I fully understand what my mother had suffered. Modern medication got me back on my feet in two weeks and spared me the two years of agony my mother knew.

There is nothing like experience to help us understand our deepest truths. What we go through in life, whether joyous or excruciating or mundane, shapes who we are and gives our life a rich fullness. Tragedy comes to all of us, in different degrees and in different forms. It doesn't feel good or fair or useful at the time. But somehow, in the great design of things, it is an intrinsic aspect of our existence that allows us to fully live.

The Son Who Learned from His Mother's Suicide

The coroners called us to remove the body of Rosalie Hart, a woman who had committed suicide. The address was in an area of large homes with wealthy residents with expensive cars in the driveway. A police officer met my co-worker Max and me at the door and said the police were still investigating the death scene. While we waited, we walked out sliding glass doors to a large patio where the whole city was spread out before us in lights. Max, a slightly built man and a chain smoker, lit his cigarette, took a drag, and said, "Wow! Is this opulence or just filthy rich?" I agreed that no one in this house seemed to lack anything money could buy.

In a few minutes we were summoned to go to the study. Seasoned as both of us were to death scenes, we were still shocked at the gory condition of the room. Rosalie Hart had aimed a 30.06 hunting rifle at her head. After tearing through her, the bullet had ricocheted, shattering the marble and glass furnishings of the study. We customarily helped to clean death scenes, but this one was formidable. As we stood there staring, the officer explained that the couple's son had come home from celebrating his upcoming twentieth birthday with friends and found his mother dead.

The officer told us the woman's husband wanted the body removed as soon as possible. Lowering his voice he whispered, "Maybe this man is in shock, but if you ask me, I think he is madder than hell about somethin'. If I were you, I'd only ask what you have to tonight."

When Max later asked Rosalie's husband, Phillip Hart, if he wished to have the body embalmed, he replied sharply, "No. I just want it cremated as soon as possible."

Phillip Hart was a tall man with a neatly trimmed beard and mustache. When he came in to make arrangements the next morning he brought his son, David. Phillip was restless, pacing the floor of the office as I tried to proceed with paperwork. When I presented him with the forms he had to sign for cremation, his anger flared and he said, "Just tell me what the bill is. I want to get the hell out of here!" No, he did not want an obituary published. No, he did not want any funeral service. No, he did not want any urn. Just use a cardboard box. I advised him he could come for the cremains on Wednesday at noon, and that is what he did, without speaking a word.

We who witness scenes such as this have many questions. Why would the wife take her own life? Why such anger in her husband? Usually our questions go unresolved. We simply move on to the next family. This time was different because David came back—ostensibly to pick up the death certificates for his father, but really he also wanted to talk to someone. As he said to me, "You see more death than I ever will, and I want to ask you some questions about what you've observed in other suicides."

In order to respond to his questions, I needed him to answer some of mine. He told me his mother met his father when she was twenty years old and modeling in New York City. After their marriage, Rosalie kept working to help her husband through law school. Phillip had been very successful as a partner in a large firm and had recently started to teach a law class at the university.

David said his childhood had been happy. His parents were devoted to each other and gave much of their time to social causes. Only within the past two years had there been a change. David thought it began when his father started teaching. He began "hanging out" with students. One day he asked David to take a suit to the cleaners for him. David checked the pockets and found a rent receipt from a new apartment complex downtown. Out of curiosity he went there and found his father's name on a mailbox corresponding to the apartment listed on the receipt.

David said, "Then I sort of tied that in with changes I had noticed at home. There were nights when Dad didn't come home, and I just thought he worked late and slept at the office. Mom and Dad quarreled more. One night I overheard her tell him that she knew he was sleeping around. They took separate bedrooms, and Mom stayed in her room a lot. With me, she was very quiet. She didn't talk to me like we always had. She stopped going to her hairdresser. Sometimes she stayed in her bathrobe all day. Dad hired a full-time housekeeper and cook, but Mom didn't seem to want much to eat, even if she came out of her room."

David explained that a month before the death, his Dad came home and announced he was planning to have about thirty of his students to the house. He wanted to show them the study he had built as his private space, with its flagstone patio from which Mount Olympus could be viewed. He also planned to exhibit some rocks, stamps, rare books, and guns from his collections.

Soon after this announcement, Rosalie showed changes. She seemed happy and had her hair and nails done professionally. She shopped, called old friends, and chatted with the housekeeper. Phillip prepared the study for his guests' viewing and gave the cook a list of food and drinks he wanted prepared. The atmosphere in the home was congenial, and David was hopeful.

However, the cook said that on the morning of the planned event, his mother called her saying that she would make preparations for that evening and the cook could have the day off. That was the last anyone heard from Rosalie Hart. That evening, the police met the guests and turned them away.

———

Unresolved grief or anger can create behavioral, mental, and health problems over time. When I learned that a memorial service was held but Phillip demanded that the ceremony be brief, I wondered if Phillip would ever seek help in dealing with his intense anger and its underlying grief. I knew that he'd been unwilling to talk anything over with his son, which was one reason why David came back to the mortuary to talk to me. At least David was looking for the help he needed to overcome his own grief.

When David came to my office, he said he wanted to apologize for his father's behavior. As a matter of fact he was puzzled by the behavior of both parents. His eyes misted up as he said, "I never dreamed anything like this could ever happen in my life. I still have a hard time believing all of this really happened." Taking a Kleenex from a box on the table, he covered his eyes and said, "I just can't figure out why she did this to me."

"I don't believe for one minute that your mother did this to hurt you," I interjected. "There are deeper issues here. In listening to you talk about your mother's self-imposed isolation, lack of appetite and loss of weight, sadness, and indifference, it reminds me of my own experience with clinical depression. And in my own case, when I was at the very bottom of depression I thought of suicide frequently. I felt like I couldn't handle the negatives anymore, and I couldn't clearly see the positives. In those moments, it seemed like it'd be easier to die than to live."

David interrupted. "But how come she was so happy for that week before she did it?"

I explained to him that I'd heard of other suicide victims who had seemed happy once they'd made the decision to kill themselves, perhaps because they feel relieved that their pain will end soon. I recommended that he seek out a grief support group at the university, and that he read *The Broken Brain,* by Nancy C. Andreasen, MD, PhD; *The Mind,* by Richard M. Restak, MD (especially chapter six, which is about depression); and *A Brilliant Madness,* by Patty Duke with Gloria Hochman (especially chapter ten, "Families Suffer and Learn").

A month later David reappeared. He carried a folder and he placed it on the table, saying, "After I left here last time I went through some of my mother's drawers in her room. I found this." He opened the folder and placed before me some newspaper clippings. As I read them, each one reported a suicide and the method used to accomplish it. Under the folder he found a copy of the book *Final Exit*, by Derek Humphry, which talks about methods of committing suicide to reduce the chances of failure.

"What do you think now?" I asked David.

"I think what you told me last time makes sense. I have spent hours at the library reading. She sure wanted to strike a pretty serious blow to my father when she did it, trashing his cherished room and also his party with his students." He hesitated and said, "Why didn't they just get a divorce?" Adding with a smile, "Or is that too simplistic?"

David told me he had joined a psychiatrist-led grief support group, through which he'd come to understand that he'd been blaming his father for everything that had happened, when really his parents had issues he knew nothing about and his position didn't require him to judge either of them. Realizing this helped him let go of having to take sides. Instead, he was now free to just focus on resolving his own pain over his damaged relationship with his father and his loss of his mother.

David went on to tell me he had moved to his fraternity house on campus. He was sleeping better and concentrating in classes seemed easier now. He thanked me and got up to leave. Standing outside, watching him walk the short distance to his car, I thought how courageous this handsome young man was to deal with his own grief and at the same time make intense efforts to understand the tragedy that had changed his life. Opening the door of his red Porsche, he raised his hand and called, "Have a nice day!"

The Newborn Whose Life Was Stolen

Max had just returned with the body of a newborn baby; we had been called to remove it from the Regis Hospital. When I took the sheet from the baby, we both gasped. Neither of us had ever seen a newborn baby covered from head to toes with dark and dried blood. This was a baby girl, weighing more than eight pounds, with rolls of fat on her arms and legs.

Max was the first to notice, "Look, she doesn't have any stump from the umbilical cord." We examined the small cavity with ragged edges where the stump should be with its usual clamp. There was little blood in the drainage as we embalmed.

The baby's father, Roy Upham, came in with his mother-in-law to make arrangements. They decided on a graveside service in two days when the mother of the baby should be able to attend. I assured them the baby would be viewable. As they were leaving, I asked Mr. Upham if he knew why the baby hadn't lived. He replied the doctor told them the cord was wrapped around her neck three times.

I repeated this to·Max. We thought this wasn't true. A baby who dies from having the cord wrapped around its neck has a well-defined neck. This baby had a small roll of fat between her head and trunk. I suddenly remembered that my Tupperware lady and next-door neighbor was also an obstetrical nurse at the Regis Hospital. I decided to purchase some Tupperware.

Betty, a widowed mother of four young children, handed me a soda as I looked through her catalogue. As usual, she was quite talkative and as she wrote my order, I said, "Betty, I took care of the Upham baby today."

"Oh, yes," she said, "I took care of Betty Upham after the delivery. It was her first baby, you know. Such a shame."

"Dr. Dixon told her husband the baby had the cord around its neck, but I don't believe that," I said to Betty.

Although we were alone in the house, she lowered her voice and leaned closer to me, "Well, the delivery room nurses said that when Dr. Dixon inserted the forceps to turn the baby, the forceps evidently got tangled in the cord and ripped it out of the umbilicus. The baby bled to death before it could be born." She paused for a moment, "He's just sick about it and we all feel so sorry for him. It was an accident."

"I know they don't allow family in the delivery room at Regis, but how did they keep the mother from knowing something was wrong?"

She told me that Dr. Dixon knew before the delivery that the baby was not in a proper position so he had an anesthesiologist helping. When both doctors recognized the problem with the baby upon delivery, the anesthesiologist sedated the mother so she would not awaken until she was in a patient room. As I drove to Dr. Dixon's office to have him sign the fetal certificate of death, I struggled with what my mortuary's responsibility was. This was an accidental death. The law is clear about reporting all accidental deaths to the coroner's office where the body would be taken and examined to determine the cause of death. The hospital and the doctor should both have reported it. Since they didn't, was I obligated to do so? Was it the right thing to do?

I entered the high-rise building and located Dr. Dixon's office on the sixth floor. I handed the blue folder containing the certificate along with my business card to the receptionist. I sat down to read a magazine. Soon a young mother carrying a newborn baby in her arms sat down near me. The baby was crying loudly and refused to be comforted. That loud raspy cry took me back to the birth of my second daughter, Lorelle. Lorelle had cried that way day and night for two years after she was born. Later she would be diagnosed with cerebral palsy; while she would have a normal intellect and go on to develop difficult but understandable speech, she would never walk and would be totally dependent for her care the rest of her life.

Lorelle was a victim of the Rh factor. She had Rh-positive blood (like her father) and mine was Rh negative, so my blood tried to destroy her blood. She was born grossly jaundiced, and the pamphlet the doctor gave me told us only how little was known about the Rh factor in 1955 (the modern-day treatment at birth had not yet come into existence).

Our physician, Chris Heber, who also happened to be my friend, couldn't do a blood exchange, which was the optimal treatment at the time. Our tiny local hospital didn't have the proper equipment. Instead, he tried to do a blood transfusion. Afterward, he apologetically told us there was a mighty fine line between enough and too much. In his attempt to save her life, he had transfused her with too much blood and put her into shock.

Because of our friendship, Chris openly admitted he had misjudged and told my husband and me we could sue him if we wanted. There were no signs of brain damage at that point. Our neurologist at UCLA Medical Center would tell us five years later that Lorelle probably had some brain damage before she was born, though he acknowledged that the after-birth treatment could have caused further damage. Medicine is not an absolute science. Had we sued Chris, it would not have healed our daughter's brain, and a conviction of malpractice in the small community we were in would have irreparably damaged the doctor's practice.

Dr. Dixon's nurse suddenly jolted me from my reverie. She called my name as she walked from her glass-enclosed cubicle to hand me the folder. I didn't open it until I got in my car. The doctor had written, "Cord around neck three times." I made my decision to leave the situation alone and simply do my work. The family had hired me to care for the disposition of the baby's body. I knew that Dr. Dixon had a large practice and was presently serving as chief of staff at the hospital where the death of the baby occurred. Both the doctor and the hospital were very much aware of the circumstances, and they had decided how they wanted to handle it. A lawsuit would give the parents money for compensation, but it would not restore their baby to life.

That afternoon I dressed that beautiful baby in a pink nylon dress with little white ducks embroidered around the hem. Mrs. Upham's mother must have worked late into the night to crochet a pink sweater with bonnet and booties to match. A pink shawl completed the outfit.

Fifty friends and family attended the graveside service. Mrs. Upham, her brown hair falling over her shoulders, was pale and walked slowly. Her husband kept a supportive arm around her. She wept during the minister's brief remarks. The group left as soon as the committal was completed. She went home without her baby.

Of the many cases I have handled, babies stir up the most emotions in me. As I watched the young mother leave the grave of her firstborn with her arms empty, my heart went out to her for not having a baby to take home after her long wait and expectations. I also felt the full intensity of my own sadness for my daughter's challenges. I never have a day that I don't think about the sadness I experienced after learning the complete diagnosis of our daughter. I also still find myself wondering how different things might have been if Chris hadn't made the mistake that he did.

I still question some of the decisions I've made in my practice. It's not always easy to tell what is in a family's ultimate best interest. But recently I had an experience that, at least for me, reaffirmed the decision I made with the Uphams. It had to do with two of my closest friends, Nonna and Marianna Kocharyan, beautiful Armenian sisters. When Ed and I toured Armenia in 1998, eighteen-year-old Nonna was our guide. We were impressed with her abilities and agreed to sponsor her as a student at Brigham Young University. Marianna followed two years later. I was with them when they received word from their brother in Armenia that their mother had committed suicide. She was fifty years old and had had schizophrenia for most of their lives.

Immediately they became hysterical, blaming each other and themselves for the death. That day and long into the night, there was much soul searching trying to find answers for this tragedy. The next day they heard from their brother again. He had had an autopsy performed and it was determined their mother died from a heart condition. They had also been able to account for her medication and could prove she had not overmedicated herself as had been initially assumed.

At hearing this news, there was an immediate lifting of a substantial part of my friends' grief. They spent that day laughing and crying as they remembered the good and the bad times with their mother. Knowing that their mother had died from a natural condition was so much easier to handle than thinking about her taking her own life.

In a similar way, I believe that for the Uphams, thinking their baby died from an act of nature was easier to handle than thinking about the forceps tearing the cord and their baby bleeding to death before she could be born.

Dr. Dixon had an accident. Chris misjudged and maybe Mother Nature did too. Both situations resulted in tragedies that can't be undone. Lorelle is now fifty years old. She receives full-time care, but there are many things about life she loves, such as music, her computer, and TV. My family, and I'm sure the Uphams, continue to deal with the consequences of those incidents and move on with our lives.

The Parents Who Finally Stopped Fighting

I was on call that weekend, and the night attendant called me at home Sunday evening to say, "A Mr. Scharf has come in and says his son is at the coroner's office. He wants us to go get him right now." I knew they wouldn't release a body after 5:00 p.m. I told Eric to ask Mr. Scharf to return the next morning. I heard the man respond, "I'll be here at ten sharp, and tell her if my son's mother comes or calls, she is not to have anything to say about this funeral. I'm in charge of everything. I have legal papers that give me full custody. Now make sure your woman understands that!"

Upon arriving at the mortuary the next morning, the secretary said I had a party of two men and four women waiting in my office. One of the women was Shirley Harrison, and she said she had come to arrange for the burial of her son, who was at the coroner's office.

With some apprehension about the complicated situation I was about to get involved in, I called the coroner's office. I found out that the boy's name was Barry McKelvey and he'd been killed in an automobile rollover. He'd been a passenger in one of two cars filled with teenagers racing on a narrow canyon road. The body had been received Sunday morning and would not be released before Tuesday. The father was Alan Scharf and the mother was, as I feared, Shirley Harrison.

Entering the office, I asked which of the women was Mrs. Harrison. A pixie-like blonde said, "Here," and flipped her long hair that had been swept to the back of her neck where it was gathered by a large clip before falling to her waist. "My son was killed in an auto accident, and I want him buried in my family's plot next to my brother and father."

Sitting, I said, "I was contacted last night by Alan Scharf, who indicted he would be assuming responsibility."

"To hell he will," she shot back with hostile eyes. "I'm the boy's mother."

"He claims he has papers granting him custody."

A black woman sitting on the couch spoke. "I'm Mrs. Johnson and I'm a friend of Mrs. Harrison. Did Mr. Scharf say what papers he has?"

"No, but he will be here at ten o'clock and he said he would bring his papers. Do you care to stay and meet with him and perhaps we can talk about this matter together?"

"I won't sit in the same room with that bastard. But I have papers, too, and you'd better not listen to him until you see mine!" said Mrs. Harrison.

"Let me talk with him and see what he has in mind."

"He's out of his mind," she snorted.

After I promised to be in touch with her as soon as I saw the papers, the sullen group stalked out of the office. Only Mrs. Johnson paused, "I hope you can help her. She's been up all night." I said I would try.

Later that morning, Alan Scharf, a tall, broad-shouldered man in his forties, tossed a folded legal-sized paper on my desk and said abruptly, "Read this." The document was issued by the Juvenile Court dated five weeks prior, granting temporary custody of Barry to his father until a court hearing on October twenty-third (which was four days hence), at which time permanent custody would be considered. Reading the papers, I felt assured that he was the one with legal responsibility for his son.

He was angry that I hadn't removed the body yet, and it wasn't until the investigator at the coroner's office talked with him that he accepted waiting another day. He said he didn't know how he would ask us to care for the body, though he said money would be no problem. If it could be viewed he wanted a viewing and services. Otherwise, he would authorize a cremation but he wanted the boy buried in his family's plot. "Now, I want one thing understood. His mother isn't to see him. Maybe I'll let her come if we have a funeral, but as you read on that paper she doesn't even have visitation privileges."

He explained that he and Shirley divorced when the boy was three years old, and he had allowed Barry's stepfather, Stan McKelvey, to adopt him because Alan worked overseas for the U.S. Government. Shirley had divorced Mr. McKelvey after having a son with him and had been married twice since then.

When I tried to talk to Mrs. Harrison, Mrs. Johnson said she was sleeping and I could leave a message with her. I told her I believed Mr. Scharf had proper authority to act, but I would need Shirley's signature on a release, as well as Mr. Scharf's and Mr. McKelvey's, before removing the body from the coroner.

Mrs. Johnson said, "Oh, I'm so sorry for her. You might as well know. She's an alcoholic and heaven only knows how she will deal with this. She's really a very nice person when she's sober and right now she's dealing with a lot of guilt, but after all, she is his mother."

Mr. McKelvey said he would fax his release directly to the coroner. I learned he had remarried after he divorced Shirley. He had full custody of his son, Brian, from the marriage to Shirley. My next call was to Shirley, asking her to bring in the papers she claimed to have and sign our release.

Late that afternoon, Mrs. Johnson came to the receptionist's desk. In a low voice she asked me, "Can you bring the paper to the car for her to sign? Shirley drank too much and fell off the porch. I think her leg is broken."

Taking the release to the car, I found Shirley moaning. With a grimace, she signed. When I asked if she brought her custody papers, she groaned, "How could I? I'm in so much pain! But I'll show you who has the right to my son. I'm going to buy him the very best." Mrs. Johnson stood near the rear of the car. She mouthed to me while shaking her head back and forth, "She hasn't got a dime." Then she went through the motions of drinking from a bottle.

When Barry's body came into the preparation room, I saw a cut over the right cheekbone, which could easily be sutured subdurally. A few abrasions should be covered cosmetically and the other wounds would be dressed and covered by clothing. There could be a viewing.

Mr. Scharf set the time for viewing on Wednesday evening, arranging for Shirley and her group to view between 5:00 and 7:00 p.m. A public viewing between 7:00 and 9:00 p.m. would be published in the obituary, at which time the father and his family would attend. In the meantime, both parents were continuing to insist that the body be interred in their respective family lots. After they each hired attorneys, I called the judge who had determined the custody of Barry. He said that he would not grant custody of a dead body to anyone and that the parents were going to have to settle that by themselves.

Our company attorney called a meeting between the parents and their attorneys, cautioning them that no burial would be conducted until the parents agreed. The next morning our attorney advised me that the parents had reached a decision. The father would have control over the funeral service and the casket selection. The mother would control the burial. Barry would be buried in the plot of her family. The father agreed to pay all expenses because Shirley couldn't. Our attorney had been helpful in convincing Alan that Shirley also had equal rights toward the care of this boy and until she was satisfied, nothing would take place. Even the judge had refused to show preferential treatment to either parent.

That Wednesday night Shirley's group was still in the room with the casket when Alan arrived with his family. Alan showed some humility as a result of the meeting with the attorneys. He invited Shirley to stay for another hour and see his family and friends, whom she hadn't seen for years. Shirley seemed happy to have more time and see old acquaintances. The viewing room was a busy place with people coming and going. Alan placed an ottoman next to a chair so Shirley could keep her leg elevated, and he brought over friends of his she hadn't met and introduced them to her.

The funeral was large. Barry had been a baseball star. There had been an article published in the local newspaper a month before naming him the high school athlete of the week. He wore his uniform in the casket and his team members came in theirs. Probably two hundred students attended. They were orderly, and a few cried.

When Mr. Scharf arrived with his group, I seated them in the family room. Soon Shirley came with her entourage and they walked slowly as Shirley moved with crutches. I took them to a back door in the chapel because the distance for her to walk was shorter. Mr. McKelvey identified himself. I seated him, his wife, and his two boys in the front row of the chapel, opposite Shirley. The overflow filled an outside court where they could hear the minister.

The grave was located two hundred yards from the chapel, so the crowd walked behind the casket to its final destination. After a brief committal, many students walked past the casket, placing on it roses, carnations, an orchid, and a bouquet of daisies. The top of the casket was completely covered with blossoms.

Barry's half-brother was the first to leave. He sobbed as he was led away by his father. Mr. Scharf left with a friend. Shirley hobbled away on crutches with her group. Her leg was in a cast up to her knee, the bone having been fractured in two places just above the ankle.

Only Shirley's elderly mother, Mrs. Johnson, and I were left at the graveside. Barry's grandmother said she had frequently cared for the two boys until she'd had to go into the hospital for her heart condition. It seemed that it was when Barry had needed her help the most that she'd had to leave.

Mrs. Johnson, a large woman in stature, wiped her eyes and said, "I'm his foster mother. I've had him three different times. I've been trying to think of a word that describes him. The one I decided on is *gentle*. That's what he was. Gentle. He never hurt nobody in his whole life. He took care of his little brother like he was his dad. It always made me happy when the social worker told me I could have him." She looked again at the casket and laid a hand on top of the flowers. "Such a lonely boy. God! How he's hurt in his sixteen years."

Slowly the two women walked arm in arm toward the gates. The autumn air was cool. The sun had remained behind the clouds all day as though it refused to shine on such a tragic day. Though at long last Barry's parents had put their grudge aside, it was impossible to forget that this reconciliation came too late to benefit him.

As the cemetery men approached the grave to complete it, it seemed appropriate that I leave too. It was something Barry had become accustomed to.

Mr. Scharf had been working in Saudi Arabia for twelve years of his son's life. Mrs. Harrison was known for partying with her friends. The boys had told social workers that their mother had left them alone for as long as three days at a time with no one to care for them. Barry assumed the care of his little brother during those times, until Mr. McElvey gained custody of his child. Barry was sent to live with foster parents on four occasions after his half-brother left.

Mr. Scharf returned home and took Barry to live with him only six weeks before the death. Reports from the Juvenile Center said Barry's behavior had changed favorably since he had a father in his life.

Studies have shown that guilt and self-blame are common in bereaved parents after the sudden loss of a child. Couples often find themselves blaming each other. Parents who were studied by psychologists reported their experience with death changed them. They learned to appraise anew what is really valuable. In this case, Barry's parents were at least able to let go of their custody battle feud, though the fact that their son was no longer around to appreciate the truce still marred this reconciliation in my mind.

This story always reminds me of the sad old joke, "I hold onto my grudges until they die of old age, then I stuff them and mount them on a pedestal." Of course, taking that approach only leads to misery and illness. Charlotte Witvliet, PhD, associate professor of psychology at Hope College in Michigan, once said that forgiveness isn't about letting offenders off easy, but about liberating the offended from the ill effects of vengefulness: "It's about letting go of the bitterness eating at us. By giving an unwarranted gift to someone who doesn't deserve it, we find out paradoxically that it is we ourselves who are freed from the bondage."

Departing Thoughts

I was working at a mortuary/cemetery combination when a fellow director rushed into my office and asked me to set up for his graveside service, which was scheduled to begin in a few minutes. He'd just noticed that the ribbon intended to top the spray of flowers on the casket was missing. He hurried to the florist nearby to have the ribbon made up with the words *Beloved Brother* on it.

The minister and the sister of the deceased were just arriving at the grave as the funeral director returned with the freshly prepared ribbon and hurriedly placed it across the casket. After the brief service, the sister approached the casket, knelt, and kissed it. Then she stood, reached for the ribbon, and paused. The director peered over her shoulder and, to his horror, read the words *Beloved Bother.*

The director apologized profusely, but the sister just laughed, saying no one had a better sense of humor than her brother and he loved a good story. She was only sorry he couldn't tell this one about himself. She wanted this ribbon to stay as it was, just to remind her of this final bit of humor at his funeral.

Trust me—that was one relieved funeral director!

Chapter Four

Learning from Our Greatest Mistakes

Mortician's Diary

I was in high school when World War II started. Many of the young men in our community left to fight the war, leaving us without enough help to harvest the crops. Dad learned from Japanese friends in Salt Lake City that some of their family needed to be rescued from the Minidoka internment camp located fifty miles from our home, so he brought three families to work on the farm, and a few other farmers in our community did the same. Dad guaranteed the government he would provide housing for the families and pay going wages for their work on the farm. The American Japanese were bright and well educated, and many of them were successful business people. The government saw fit to remove them from all coastal areas and confine them in the camps until the end of the war. They held Saturday-night dances and invited the community to come. The fellows were good dancers and my sister and I had a good time when we attended.

Before the war was over, several of the young Japanese men volunteered to fight in Italy. The ones who came home had been awarded medals, and their division received much public praise for their outstanding achievements in battle. Three of the eight did not return. When the families went home to Seattle after VJ Day, their greenhouses had been flattened and every glass broken. They rebuilt in the face of continued discrimination. Two years later, Akiko, the young father of one family, was found unconscious with his head on the running board of his floral van. The police assumed he was drunk, so they transferred him to a jail cell. His wife found him after searching all night. She had him transferred to a hospital where he soon died from the stroke that had been left untreated.

This wasn't the only time I witnessed tragedies occurring because of discrimination. In 1944, I was studying at the Cincinnati College of Mortuary Science. At first, I was the only woman in a class made up of a few medically discharged military men and several men who were classified 4-F by the draft. Six months later we were joined by sixty additional medically discharged men, as well as one more woman.

Four of my classmates were black, which was new for me as a young woman from Idaho who hadn't even seen a black person until I was sixteen years of age. I found that I got along well with these four men, especially one young man who came from a wealthy family that owned a large mortuary in Georgia. One day he called and asked me to go with him to a concert presented by the Cincinnati Symphony Orchestra with Oscar Levant as soloist. I would have loved to attend that event, but I declined because I already had a steady boyfriend.

The next morning, I naively mentioned the call to my North Carolinian boyfriend as we chatted about the events of the previous day. He made no comment, but the following day I was called to the dean's office, where I was told that my boyfriend had told four other white, Southern classmates about the call, and that they had made a plan to lynch my friend as a result. After explaining that my black friend had been sent home to Georgia for a year for his safety, the dean proceeded to explain that things were different in Ohio than they were in Idaho. I learned that day that my own innocent mistake could have resulted in the death of an innocent man. I also became more fully aware of the level of intolerance in my community.

Our country has a bountiful history of intolerance and oppression. As I look back over my long and varied life, I wonder how much our nation has learned from our greatest mistakes. Tragedies happen, both in our society and in our personal lives, and there's nothing we can do to change the past. Sometimes in life the only thing we can do is learn enough from our mistakes that we don't make the same ones again.

The Father Who Didn't Appreciate His Little Girl in Time

They were a disheveled, exhausted pair when they came in to arrange for the burial of their four-year-old daughter,

Merrie. I showed them to my office, and as the wife talked, I learned that their names were Eric and Deena Larson. They lived in a rural part of Salt Lake City where Mr. Larson operated a small produce farm. One of the three stands he operated was located about a mile from our mortuary, and I often purchased fruits and vegetables there, especially corn. He had six tow-headed sons, ranging in age from six to fifteen, who he paired off to operate each outlet. The young boys were well mannered and efficient and their wares were always fresh, as well as beautifully displayed.

Deena told me that Merrie, their only daughter, had followed her puppy when it ran into the street in front of their home. When she dashed after him, both were hit by an oncoming car. The puppy was killed instantly, and Merrie had been rushed to the hospital where she lived for three days following brain surgery because of a fractured skull.

Eric sat slumped in a wing chair, staring ahead. He spoke only once during our hour together. He told his wife, "Do whatever you want." Deena sat in a chair next to him never letting go of his hand. She explained that Merrie's long blonde hair had been shaved off in the hospital, but that her neighbor was a beautician and would get a raw wig and style it whenever I gave her an appointment to come.

As she talked, Eric slumped over with his head in his wife's lap. His shoulders convulsed with sobs. Deena stroked his curly brown hair as she said gently, "Cry all you want to, my darling. I love you." Then she said to me "He's been so supportive of me at the hospital these past horrible days. I have cried myself dry on his shoulder. Now it's his turn. He was so sure she would live. We prayed so hard. Now she's gone—I have to help him." He sat up holding a tissue over his eyes. I promised to call them and set a viewing time once I could determine what restoration would be necessary.

I was alarmed when the body came from the coroner. The wig would cover the incision from the surgery and the purple areas on the child's bare head. It wouldn't be as easy to cover the dark purple areas surrounding her eyes, or the jagged tear, now debrided and sutured, where her mouth had been wounded. Abrasions covered much of her face. Max and I decided to remove the plaster cast from her right arm, embalming the arm so it would lie straight by her side.

The next morning the hairdresser styled the wig with bangs and softly curled the ends that fell over the child's shoulders. As we finished the cosmetics, Max restored a few scattered freckles over the little turned-up nose. We dressed her in a long-sleeved white blouse covered by a red-and-white checked gingham pinafore. We finished by placing under Merrie's left arm a sleeping baby doll dressed in a white, lace-trimmed nightgown. It was a perfect touch.

When Deena saw Merrie she showed marked relief, saying, "Thank God I can remember her like this." Eric sank into the nearest overstuffed chair, chanting over and over, "Oh, God, why did this have to happen?" He remained thusly for the rest of the evening, speaking only to their pastor.

The next day I directed a brief graveside service. The pastor, holding his Bible in his long, slender fingers, read, "Jesus said: Suffer little children, and forbid them not, to come unto me: for of such is the kingdom of heaven." He counseled those assembled to remember that the quality of life was more important than the quantity. In conclusion, he said, "She was a loving child. She was a model child. We all sorrow over the fact that she has been taken from us after four brief years, but we also should rejoice that God, in His wisdom, gave her to us to love and to cherish for these four wonder-filled years."

Tears ran down Eric's broad, sun-tanned cheeks. Deena held his hand. Their six white-haired sons gathered around them like stepping stairs.

As the family walked to their car, Eric laid his arm around his wife's shoulders and she swept her arm around his waist. Helping her into the station wagon, he glanced back at the small casket with its spray of velvet-like red roses. He wiped his eyes again while the boys found their places in the seats behind their mother.

A week later I stopped at the produce stand where Gordon, the third Larson son, sorted through a pile of corn to find six good ears for me while I selected some tomatoes. His little brother scampered to right a price card that had been toppled by a breeze. "How is everyone at your house this week?" I asked casually.

"It's sure different without Merrie around. It's really been hard on Dad. Mom says it will take time and lots of love to help him." He was a polite boy, smiling and chatting as he carried the bag of produce to my car and opened the door for me.

Several days passed, until one morning, soon after I unlocked the front door, Eric Larson walked in. His clothes and hands were dirty. A sweaty lock of hair had fallen onto his forehead. I motioned for him to sit down but he sighed and said, "You wouldn't believe me if I told you where I've been."

"Why don't you try me?"

"I've been at Merrie's grave all night. I tried to dig her up with my bare hands." I looked down at his mud-caked hands. One finger had a cut on it. "Too many rocks," he muttered. He looked toward the room where Merrie's body had been viewed. "Can I go sit in there? I won't stay long. I just want to be alone for a few minutes where I saw her for the last time."

I agreed, and after a while he came back to my desk, tears streaming down his face. Bitterly he said, "I'd give anything if I could have her back." He slammed the rock wall by my desk with his fist. A small area on the side of his hand started to bleed. With obvious anger he shoved the wounded area into his mouth and bit it as he turned abruptly and left.

I was at a loss to figure this man out. I had watched grieving fathers before, but never one who seemed quite this tormented.

A month later, a woman named Mrs. Harris came in to have us take care of her elderly mother, who had died in a nursing home. She maneuvered about in the chair trying to settle her large body comfortably. She finally perched her folded hands on top of her arched stomach and leaned back. She gave me her address, which I recognized immediately. I asked, "Do you live near the Larson family?"

She smoothed the split ends of her bleached hair, "Why, yes, they live next door. That's the reason I came here. Anybody who could fix up that little girl like you did can have my business." I thanked her and told her I had been concerned about them.

"Well, Deena's a brick. Eric is taking it hard, but then he should. I don't feel sorry for him one bit. He's no man! He's an animal! Merrie was the sweetest child that ever lived, but do you know what I heard him say to her? He said, 'Little girls aren't good for anything. I needed another boy.' Now, how do you thank that made her feel?"

She continued, "Then another time he sent her to chase a calf out of the tomatoes. She got frightened and ran back to him crying. She lifted up her arms to him asking to be held and do you know what he said to her? I was standing behind the ivy. He couldn't see me but I could see him. He said, 'It's bad enough you're a girl, but you don't have to be dumb, too!' Can you imagine? A cute little girl like that! No-siree. I can't stand him!"

I'd heard everything I needed to know to finally understand this father's anguish. I reached for my pen. "Mrs. Harris, will you please spell your mother's first name?"

———

I read a statement recently by an anonymous author: "We have been so anxious to give our children what we didn't have that we neglected to give them what we did have." I thought of Eric Larson when I read it. He was consumed by making a living, and his sons were a big part of that. It seemed that the children in that family were valued primarily for what they could contribute to the family income. Sometimes when we do something hurtful and we can't take it back, we feel such intense guilt that we attempt to punish ourselves as a way to right our past wrongs. But the self-inflicted wounds on Eric's hands and in his heart weren't going to help Merrie or anyone else in their family. This kind of destructive guilt doesn't solve problems, it just creates more pain. When morticians see this behavior in family members, we often recommend that they seek a professional therapist to help resolve the inner distress. It was my hope for this family that Eric would learn and grow from this death. Events such as this help most of us to mature, becoming more aware of the fragility of life and better appreciating our loved ones while they're still with us.

The Teen Who Fell from Grace

In the Tuesday morning newspaper, I read an article about a pregnant teenager who was killed in an accident at a home for unwed mothers. During the night she'd fallen from a third-story window onto a cement patio, breaking her neck. The body was found when a gardener arrived for work soon after daylight. The paramedics, arriving on the scene soon after the discovery, determined the baby she was carrying was also dead. Because of her age, her name was not disclosed.

After arriving at work on Wednesday, the secretary informed me I was scheduled to meet with José and Lucia Santos at 11:00 a.m., saying only that their daughter had been killed in an accident.

Once they arrived and introductions had been made, I learned that their deceased seventeen-year-old daughter's name was Maria. She was the girl mentioned in the newspaper article. They also explained that their family came from Brazil, and that Mr. Santos owned his own import-and-export business. They had lived in Orange County for twelve years and spoke English well, though they still conversed with each other in Portuguese. They had three daughters, and Maria was the middle child.

Lucia was a stunning woman with olive skin, dressed in a calf-length silk dress and high-heeled boots reaching to her knees. She cried often during the hour we were together, and she seemed irritable when she and her husband spoke in their native tongue. The lines in his face made him look stern, and he gave me the impression that he was always in charge as he tried to negotiate every price I quoted. Both his manner and his tailored brown suit seemed to fit his role as a very successful businessman.

Before they left I asked Lucia about clothing for Maria, and she said she would bring in the cheerleading outfit from school. I hadn't seen the body so I asked, "In what stage of her pregnancy was your daughter?" Lucia said, "She was due next week." She broke into sobs. I told her the baby would come to us from the coroner wrapped in a flannel blanket, so she might consider bringing us a receiving blanket and we would place the baby inside the foot of the casket.

When the body arrived I knew the cheerleading suit was not an option. I called Lucia and suggested she look for a tent dress, which was popular in 1982. I recommended that she choose a rich fabric and subdued color with a piece of bright jewelry to take attention away from the added weight around the abdominal area.

Maria's college-aged sister, Alexandra, brought the clothing to me, and it was from her that I learned that the pregnancy had been kept a secret. Friends and family members had been told that Maria was away at a private school for a year. The plan was to place the baby for adoption.

Alexandra, a tall girl with delicate features, waited while I dressed the body. After looking at her sister's remains and approving, she called her mother to come. The dress and jewelry had worked magic and Maria was beautiful. As soon as Lucia viewed her daughter, she appeared ready to collapse so we helped her to a chair. As she fanned her mother, Alexandra said to me, "This is so hard for Mother. This baby is her grandchild, but Father said he would not be humiliated this way. He said Maria had disgraced the whole family and this baby had to go." She asked me what sex the baby was. When I told her it was a boy, Lucia's cries grew louder.

The chapel was filled to capacity for the service. Most of those attending were students from the high school Maria attended. A young man who appeared a bit more mature than the students sat on the back row holding his head in his hands. In concluding the services I invited those who wished to say a final farewell to file past the casket. The young man in the back row remained seated until nearly everyone had viewed, then he stepped forward and those remaining in the line stepped aside to let him go first. He went outside using a handkerchief to wipe his eyes. I wondered if he might be the father of the baby. As I overheard conversations among those in the line, I learned this baby was not really a secret from these students. Lucia's two daughters supported her as she left the chapel crying. Jose was alone in the chapel. He stepped to the casket and his shoulders shook from sobs. Waiting a moment to regain his usual stoic composure, he went to the car.

I stood in the exit of the parking lot waving the cars into a line to go to the cemetery. A man in a suit approached me and asked me quietly, "What was the baby?" He looked like he might be in his forties with graying temples. I was surprised, but I quickly figured he was a grandfather or he wouldn't know to inquire. I responded it was a boy. I told him the truth when he asked me where the baby was. Then he said, "We are so sorry it ended like this. The kids really wanted to keep the baby. My wife and I were prepared to help them. They would have grown up fast as parents, and I know it could have worked."

He went on to explain that while Maria was at home for a visit the previous week, she had somehow managed to call his son on the phone and they planned for her to climb out of her window, crawl along a ledge to some stairs and unlock the gate. "My son waited all night near his car for Maria to come hoping to drive to Las Vegas and have the baby there. They planned to get married as soon as she had her next birthday and be a family. Lucia favored the marriage, but Jose is a very proud man."

Before he left he handed me an envelope. "There's $4,000 in here. We know we bear responsibility in this, too. Please keep it anonymous. Thanks for what you have done."

I caught up with the group at the cemetery. After the benediction and in keeping with the tradition of many Latin people, two men took the shovels standing up in the pile of dirt to be used in filling the grave. They each poured a shovel of dirt into the grave. At the sound of the clods of dirt hitting the vault, Lucia started to cry again and her daughters escorted her to their car. As people began to leave, Jose took a shovel of dirt, emptied it into the grave, then another, after which he attacked the pile of dirt ferociously, shoveling one mound after the other. The priest who stood watching soon stepped forward, removed the shovel from Jose's hands and put his arm around his shoulders. Jose turned and sobbed on the shoulder of the robed man. The priest talked in low tones to him as they walked toward the waiting limousine, and Lucia reached out her hand to support Jose as he joined the women in the car.

———

Lucia and her two daughters were unhappy with Jose and blamed him for Maria's death. Even the paternal grandfather of the baby said Jose was a man with pride. Maybe too much. Occasionally, I wonder what happened to this family and if the damage done to the relationship between Jose and his family was ever healed.

Sometimes we worry so much about our reputation that we put what others think before what's really important in life: the people we love most. If Jose hadn't been so worried about what people thought, he would have had his daughter, a son-in-law, and a baby grandson in his life. Instead, he was left with only a family who resented the dire cost of his pride and rigidity.

The Parents Who Rejected Their Son
in Life Missed His Death

It was early in the 1980s that AIDS came into our awareness, causing anxiety and fear among many. The men on our staff who removed bodies from the place of death suddenly refused to touch dead bodies if there was the slightest chance AIDS might be involved in the death. The men who refused more than once were dismissed, and the ones who stayed donned gloves and white gowns that were destroyed as soon as the remains were placed on a preparation table or in a cool room to await cremation.

Since we were located in the Hollywood area, we soon started holding funerals for AIDS victims, and we increasingly saw single gay men and gay couples coming in to make prearrangements for themselves. Such was the case when Gary and Boyd, a couple in their forties, presented themselves at our office.

Gary was tall, thin, and pale. He had been diagnosed with AIDS several months before and he looked ill. Boyd, on the other hand, was shorter, stocky, and had rosy cheeks to go with his reddish-blond hair. Boyd had been told he was HIV positive. They both wanted to prearrange their funerals, though I could already tell that Gary's would be happening long before Boyd's.

Perhaps that was why Boyd agreed to complete paperwork first, to soften the blow for his dying partner. He gave me his vital statistics, said he preferred to be cremated, and then said that the service details could be decided by his parents or sister. He prepaid into a trust fund the necessary cost. At the end, he handed me the Durable Power of Attorney forms that both he and Gary had completed and signed before an attorney, giving the surviving member of the two total power to control assets and make decisions for the deceased. This was essential, as without it the final decisions would be left to the next of kin. The significant other would be left with no control.

When it was Gary's turn, I asked if Gary's family would also take part in planning his services. I had unwittingly opened Pandora's Box. "My family hates me," Gary said with great emotion. "When I told my parents I was gay, they disowned me. Dad said he never wanted to see me again. No son of his would be queer. My mother agreed. She said I had embarrassed them long enough. It would be better for everyone if I never came home again."

Boyd touched Gary's hand and said, "He has my family now. My parents and my sister and her husband and kids love both of us as we are."

In completing the papers for Gary's pre-need, he asked that his body be cremated and the cremains scattered at sea. He stipulated that no one was to be allowed to view his body at any time and that no services were to be held. Boyd agreed to this on paper.

Five months later Boyd called and said Gary had passed away. I had all of the necessary paperwork and the costs had been prepaid, but I asked Gary if he would mind coming in to sign an authorization for the cremation. Although I had Gary's signature, I generally tried to get additional authorization from the person in charge. I also sensed that Boyd could use someone to talk to who understood his loss and accepted him as he was.

When he came in, I remarked how well he looked. He said his HIV had not progressed measurably and he felt good. He added, "I cared for Gary at home until he died. Our friends helped and the doctor was wonderful to see that we had all the medications we needed. The last couple of weeks Gary couldn't eat and lost even more weight." After he signed the cremation papers, he mentioned that Gary's mother had come from Idaho the previous week. "She called and asked to see him. It was hard for me to tell her she couldn't, but Gary insisted she not come to the house."

"She was unhappy when I told her 'no' because she said she had rights as a mother. I told her that I held Gary's Durable Power of Attorney and that gave me the right to refuse her. Then I thought I might as well get it over with and I told her she wouldn't be able to see him after the death."

I asked him how she responded to that. He said, "She told me she was going to hire an attorney." Both Gary and I knew exactly what the attorney told her. Gary had friends and our mortuary staff had served residents of this community before who had encountered this same issue. The attorney undoubtedly advised her that the Durable Power of Attorney holder would prevail. Even if she had wanted to pursue the chancy venture of trying to get the Durable Power of Attorney overruled in court, she would have been advised that it would take months to get a hearing. By then, Gary's body would already be cremated and scattered at sea. Like so many other unaccepting family members in her situation, she had wasted years in which she could have resolved this problem with her son.

The next day Gary's mother came to the mortuary and asked with some defiance to see her son. I showed her my papers with Gary's signature stating he didn't want his body viewed by anyone. With resignation she asked me to order two certified copies of the death certificate. She said she needed one for an insurance policy Gary had given to her to repay her for purchasing a car for him when he was younger. He also had a small savings account he probably forgot he had. She needed to close it. She paid for the certificates and left.

I learned that Gary's mother reported me to the Board of Embalmers and Funeral Directors for being rude and refusing to let her view the body of her son when a representative from the board came to my office and interviewed me. Before he left, the state board representative concluded that I had handled the situation well. He commented, "These are difficult cases we handle these days.

Gary and Boyd were only the first of many disputes we would see between family members and significant others. Any gay man who called us to request care for a companion was always asked first, "Do you have a Durable Power of Attorney?" And even though most of them did, these careful legal measures didn't protect surviving partners from painful conflicts with their partner's family members.

The gay and lesbian people we cared for had great support systems within their own communities. The funeral services were well attended and the grief of their friends was just as genuine and caring as that of the families I served. And yet I couldn't help but feel for those departed whose families had abandoned them, and for the families who were missing out on saying goodbye to their own sons and daughters.

I was not rude to Gary's mother. In many ways, I felt sorry for her. This mother lost her son twice—once by her own rejection and then by his death. Undoubtedly she grieved both times. The second time was probably more difficult because at that point she had no hope for resolution with her son. Still, I had to be firm in adhering to Gary's signed wishes in the pre-arrangement and respecting Boyd's legal rights. I know she was angry—maybe most at herself for the decision she made years ago. I just happened to be the recipient of some of her anger, and the state board representative knew that.

All of us have to live with decisions we've made, and sometimes we make decisions that are ill informed or without thought of possible consequences. When Gary's parents disowned him, I don't think his father realized that he would die without having ever made peace with his son. I don't think his mother considered that she might be denied the privilege of sitting at her son's deathbed or viewing his body. I don't think they thought about the pain they were bringing on their son and themselves. Sometimes in life we learn things the hardest way.

Departing Thoughts

The newly widowed Mrs. Nordham brought in her husband's clothing for his burial. As I took the garment bag from her, she said, "May I look at the selection of dresses you have in the casket display room?" I escorted her to the room, where she started examining each dress. I was curious, but I said nothing. Finally, she picked out a pink dress with frilly lace and jeweled buttons, handed it to me, and said, "I feel that I have to do this. Nine years ago, you folks buried my mother in a dress that fit her like a sack. She was always so neat and fussy about her clothing that I can't get that image of her out of my mind. When you close Cal's casket after the viewing, I want you to put this dress over his arm and he will take it to her. She will like this and it will fit."

After calmly agreeing to her request, I took the clothing, including the dress, to the dressing room. As I labeled it, John entered. He was our seventy-eight-year-old weekend attendant, and his claim to fame was that he'd embalmed Clark Gable. He lived all week to come in and help in many little ways and keep in touch with the staff. As he watched me label both the dress and suit with the name of *Nordham,* his bushy white eyebrows shot up. I said, "You won't believe this, John, but I am going to tell you anyway." As I finished the explanation, he started to laugh. His laughter rolled into a roar, and I worried about him keeping his standing balance. As his laughter subsided, he reached for a monogrammed handkerchief and wiped the tears running down his cheeks.

"Tell me," he said, "My mother always loved white Wonder Bread. When I die will you put a loaf in my arms to take to her?" "Sure I will, but unless you change your arrangements to be cremated, she can't even expect charred toast!"

Chapter Five

Celebrating Life

Mortician's Diary

Cemeteries have always fascinated me, perhaps because I see them as a celebration of life, rather than ghostly reminders of the past. As a child visiting our small city cemetery in Idaho, I was intrigued with the Japanese section's strange decorations. Often food was at the head of the graves, and we children were not above eating the fresh fruit before the birds did. Rest assured our parents never knew.

That cemetery always felt like a safe and peaceful place. Even when the Teton dam broke on the Snake River in 1976, the raging river only lapped at the bottom row of graves and did not sweep away any caskets or vaults—though it destroyed nearly every building in its path. Many survivors of that disastrous flood found their refuge on the hill inside the burial grounds.

Later in my life, when my first husband and I traveled with our three girls, my daughters called cemeteries "Mother's Disneyland." They never explained that to me, but soon they walked with me and looked at the pictures and took an interest in the inscriptions.

In addition to a safe haven, I've always seen cemeteries as tributes to the lives of real people. They remind me to take stock of my own life by telling me stories about the lives of others and the history of those who came before me. While traveling through Kirtland, Ohio, in the summer of 1964, my family stopped to eat lunch in an old cemetery. As I walked among the markers, I found five graves that held the remains of five brothers who died between the ages of fifteen and twenty-eight. All of them were killed on battlefields in the Civil War. I paused to think of that conflict and of the sacrifices made by just one family, and suddenly a long-ago fight felt personal and real. The girls gathered 'round while my husband and I talked about the war and the controversy at that time.

Some cemeteries are designed explicitly to memorialize the victims of large-scale atrocities in human history, and visiting these sites often makes a distant historical event feel immediate and emotional. In 1997, my husband Ed and I visited an old synagogue and cemetery in downtown Prague. The small burial area next to the synagogue was a mass of upright headstones made from sandstone, most of them two feet or more in height, but each stone only had one name on it. We were told that each grave had an average of ten bodies interred in it. The remains had been buried without caskets or vaults over a period of many years. Each grave had as many headstones as space would allow. We walked on a small path that meandered wherever there was clearance.

Going inside the synagogue we found all of the interior walls telling their own story of horror. Horizontal lines an inch apart had been drawn on every wall, and written in those small spaces were the names of 750,000 Jews from Prague who died in the Holocaust. Those bodies were buried or cremated at the whim of the Nazis. The names we stood reading were their only public memorial. Workers were still writing names and dates as we watched. A guide explained that all of the walls had been covered this way previously but vandals had entered and rendered all names unreadable by spraying paint randomly. Thus they were being done a second time. It seemed like evil had been heaped upon evil, and I wondered when it would stop, if ever.

We also visited the National Memorial Cemetery of the Pacific of Honolulu, where thousands of white crosses marked, among others, the graves of many victims of Pearl Harbor. We went on a Memorial Day, and each grave was outlined with at least one lei of fresh flowers made for that day by school children. The many leis, plus plants and wreaths, made it a sea of colors. We spent three hours taking in the colorful and vast memorial, as a huge crowd of visitors and cars inched ahead commemorating those who were gone.

When I travel in foreign countries, I try to visit a cemetery in each large city. I feel that it gives me a better sense of the culture and history of the people and places. In 1998, Ed and I viewed a cemetery that extended for many acres in Gumri, Armenia. Gumri was the center of a 1988 earthquake of 8.0

magnitude that leveled most buildings. More than five hundred thousand people were left homeless and many thousands were killed, most of whom were buried in the cemetery we viewed. Because the inscriptions were written in Armenian, I could not read any of the thousands of stone memorials that marked the acres of graves, but the vastness of the new interments was overwhelming. The numerous Armenians we knew in Los Angeles had taught us they were Christian and very traditional people who remained close to their families and their origins.

In Beijing Ed and I meandered through an ancient burial ground on the side of a steep hill. A family could inter or entomb more than fifty cremains in a four-by-four-foot space that went below the ground, and yet other spaces had walls built on them that reached seven feet in the air. Space was precious in that area and demanded that it be utilized wisely. All writing was foreign to us so we couldn't read the inscriptions, although it appeared that some were utilized by numerous cremains, perhaps twenty-five. Others were relatively bare. We saw food placed beside many memorials, but by that time I had the respect for this custom that it deserved. I hope the souls who returned for sustenance received it, as their surviving loved ones intended.

While strolling with Ed through another cemetery in Prague, I took note of the rows of graves where nuns were buried; planted flowers and picket fences marked their section separately and cloistered them in death much as they had chosen to be in life. Similarly, there were rows of graves designated for priests, which were decorated with mosaics and had crosses as head markers. This section was much more ornate with gold and marble in the decorations and surrounded by a sturdy brick wall.

Another section seemed to be for more secular residents but evidently with status and/or wealth in their communities. Glass-enclosed shelves that displayed photos and other mementos occupied their marble headstones. There were pieces of jewelry, a small booklet, and some statue items that looked like they could be awards given for honors. In talking with a groundskeeper he said they had never had problems with theft or vandalism. I thought this display was much more meaningful than the way we place our mementos inside of caskets before burial.

Sometimes it's just average people with average gravestones that affect me the most deeply and personally. When Ed and I visited Auckland, New Zealand, in 1996, we could see from our hotel window many large trees with branches sweeping toward the ground. Tall shrubs were hiding what we discovered later to be an old cemetery. As we walked among the broken and tipped headstones surrounded by tall grass, we read what we could from the sandstone markers that the forces of nature had rendered almost illegible. One marker noted the man buried there had died in 1884 at the age of thirty-five. His inscription said, "He endured many years of affliction with much patience and resignation." I wondered what illness this man had known, and I felt a kinship with him as the marker resonated with my own daughter's struggle with cerebral palsy.

Before working in cemeteries, I viewed them as beautiful, serene shrines. Since working in them, I also envision all that lies beneath the vibrant green sod—electric connections, water lines, markers placed by surveyors who measure each grave to the inch. I wonder where the sandy areas are that cause sides of graves to collapse as they are dug, and whether an area has high water tables or spots of the hard-pan that requires small dynamite explosions to open a grave. When I see open spaces in newer cemeteries, I note the young saplings that will grow tall and fill (and I mean *fill*) the as-yet unoccupied lots with roots.

Whenever I visit a cemetery, I also think back over all the things that I've learned about living through my work with death. My first opportunity to work in a cemetery came in 1970 in Salt Lake City, Utah, when we moved there to accommodate my husband's work. With my options still limited as a woman in the field, I took a job as a pre-need counselor at Riverside Estates, which had plans for a new mortuary on the drawing board in addition to owning three cemeteries in various stages of development. I saw this as an opportunity for me to learn about another area of the death care industry, but I found it more challenging than I'd expected. I had always worked in a mortuary where people needed our services when they came in. I was now in a position of convincing people to buy something they wouldn't need until they died.

When families came in to arrange for a burial, I started asking for names and addresses of other family members hoping they might be interested in purchasing graves near the deceased. Other salespeople envied me because these leads were more fruitful than "cold leads" from door-to-door or phone solicitation. I kept a card file on each lead where I recorded my contacts and the prospective customer's response. I was accumulating many cards and not selling as much as my manager, John Bywater, thought I should. Mr. Bywater was a kind but firm mentor when it came to my production.

He called me to his office one morning, asking me to bring my box of cards with me so we could review them together. The first card we looked at was Charles Justing. We had buried his father-in-law six weeks before. I recorded four telephone contacts with Charles in which he had repeatedly stated that his wife wanted two graves next to her father. But each time I tried to make an appointment to visit him, he gave me an excuse and a promise he would buy. The first time he said his wife was still upset over her father's death. The next time they planned on being out of town for two weeks. The third time he said his wife was having her period and that wasn't a good time to approach her. The fourth time he made an appointment for me to meet him at his home; upon arriving there at the scheduled time, I found no one home.

After I finished relaying these details, John said to me,

"June, I count four promises this man has made to you. How many bills have you paid this past month with promises?" That was a new way for me to think about sales.

I reached Mr. Justing that evening to tell him I would hold the lots for two weeks. After that they would be put back on the market. He made an appointment to come in the next day; he kept it and purchased four spaces instead of two. I learned that day that even when it comes to preparing for death, there is wisdom in making necessary decisions and then moving on with life.

The Woman Who Found Amazing Grace

I first met Grace Petersley and her husband, Jay, in 1971 during a house call I made to give them information on our cemetery programs. They lived in a red brick home in an upper middle-class section of Salt Lake City. Jay greeted me at the front door. He was in his mid-forties, moderately obese, and graying at his temples. Grace looked and laughed like Gracie Allen. Her mark of distinction was a stylish blonde wig. I later learned that she owned several, and she always curled and combed her own blonde hair before donning her wig for the day.

Upon concluding my presentation, they seemed interested. I did note that Jay made all of the decisions and Grace sat quietly, seemingly endorsing them. They liked my idea of asking other family members to buy lots with them, making it a family plot. They asked for time to contact their three married children who lived in the city.

The following week, I returned and wrote contracts for six spaces. Their two sons came with their wives and we finalized the paperwork that night. Again, Jay controlled the evening and the sons were compliant with his wishes. We visited for a pleasant hour while Grace served pineapple-upside-down cake topped with whipped cream. Noting her warmth as a mother and her charm as a hostess, I knew I wanted to know her better.

Two weeks later, I called Grace on a weekday, when I knew Jay would be at work, and said I would be in her neighborhood around 11:00 a.m. When I asked if I could drop off their cemetery deeds, she readily agreed and offered to fix lunch.

That day Grace and I spent a pleasant hour learning more about each other and discovered we had a lot in common. Foremost, we both had controlling husbands and we did not enjoy it. Grace described herself as a prisoner of love. She said, "Since the day I married Jay, I have never had as much as a thin dime in my purse. Don't misunderstand me," she continued. "Jay is very generous in his own way. He will take me anywhere I want and buy me anything I ask for, but he will not let me have any money of my own or any knowledge of our finances." He had never let her learn to drive, and he didn't like it when she went anywhere without him. Occa-sionally their daughter would take her out, but only with Jay's permission.

I was not a captive in the same manner, but whenever I wanted to express myself creatively I was equally a prisoner. For example, when I decided to make a mosaic table, I was confined to my husband's choice of design and tile color. When the tiles I glued to the table under a teacher's direction didn't please him, he chiseled them off. I shelved the project and never returned to it. Our husbands also dictated how we did our housework: Jay insisted that Grace scour the sink and bathtubs each time they were used. I was required to have two ounces of Lysol for each gallon of mop water. We both knew retribution for noncompliance. Both of us had experienced verbal chastisement, and I had known an occasion of physical assault because of his anger.

Divorce was not an option for either of us at the time. Grace did not have necessary skills for making a living, having married soon after graduating from high school. My disabled daughter required more attention than I could give her and provide for her financially if I was single. We both felt trapped, and being able to commiserate solidified our friendship.

Two years later, at one of our regular lunches at her house, Grace confided to me that she was hemorrhaging and was planning to have a hysterectomy. For years she had suffered from endometriosis. Her doctor explained to her that if the pain was to be relieved, he would also have to remove the ovaries and a surgical menopause would result. After the surgery, I took her some flowers. I found her depressed. Jay had spoken to the doctor before the surgery, voicing his disapproval of the whole procedure. He understood that a woman's libido was often diminished in a surgical menopause. He did not want anything that might jeopardize his sex life. In order to placate him the doctor had only removed the uterus to stop the hemorrhaging but left the ovaries—also leaving Grace with the pain of endometriosis.

A year later Grace had to have the second surgery to gain relief from pain. She had gained the courage to defy his wishes by simply telling him their daughter would take her to the hospital. When I visited her after the surgery, she seemed to be in better spirits and she said with a smile, "I made this up just for your benefit: I am so mad at Jay for what has happened that I couldn't warm up to him again if we were cremated together!" We laughed, though we both knew what she was saying was true: She would never forgive him for putting his pleasure over her pain.

Two years later, Jay died. I learned of his death from our secretary, who called me from the office and said Grace and her son wanted to meet with me at 2:00 p.m. to make funeral arrangements. The cause of death on the death certificate was *myocardial infarction*. A heart attack. He died at home.

The arrangements with Grace and her son were routine. To each choice she said she couldn't afford the best but he deserved better than the least, so each item was moderately priced. She finally had access to their financial information: Jay carried $60,000 in life insurance, and he had no debts.

Two days after the funeral, I stopped by Grace's home with her certified copies of the death certificate. She had a sandwich waiting for me, and she talked about Jay's passing. She said, "His death is a shock to me because we thought he had good health, but we both knew he was too heavy and he didn't like to exercise."

I asked her if she had any plans. "Oh, yes," she said. "Within twenty-four hours of his death, I knew what I would do. I'm starting driving lessons next week, for starters." Grace was forty-nine, one year younger than her husband. She'd been living under his rule for thirty years.

As soon as she got her driver's license, she attended business college to learn secretarial skills. A year later she got a position as a secretary to a loan officer in a bank in downtown Salt Lake City. She then enrolled in night classes at the University of Utah, bent on getting her degree in business administration. Upon accomplishing that, she was named the senior loan officer at the same bank. She ended up working there for fifteen years before retiring.

She enjoyed traveling and her grandchildren. A few years ago, I had lunch with her during a layover in Los Angeles before she traveled to Greece. She was going to stay there for several months to visit with distant relatives and collect a history of her own roots. She was enthused about the journey. As we parted, she said, "I feel so ambivalent; there were parts of marriage I really miss, like children and social life with a companion, but there are other parts about being single that I love. I am my own person and I can do my own bidding and not feel selfish about it. It is liberating but also lonely at times." She shrugged her shoulders, "But it's my life and I'm happy the way it is."

Fernando De Rojas, who lived in the fourteenth century, wrote, "When one door closes, fortune will usually open another." That door was opened for Grace.

~

It is not uncommon for a survivor to feel relief when experiencing the death of one who is close to them; many caregivers who have served for long illnesses of loved ones or survivors of difficult relationships are examples. One man told me his mother, who died at the age of 101, quoted from the Bible, saying, "I know how Job felt when he said, 'My soul is weary of life.'"

After twenty-one years of marriage, six years after Grace's liberation, I gave up waiting for my first husband to exit my life and simply went through the courts for a divorce in 1976. Lorelle graduated from high school, and California had much better programs for her. She could now go into a home in the community to live with other cerebral palsy adults, and college would be available to her if she wished. She was twenty years old and wanted to be on her own. Lorelle and I returned to Los Angeles to live, where I had a job waiting for me with the same company where I began my career in 1945. My other daughters were independently attending college. I could now manage alone.

The Husband Who Finally Let His Wife's Life Be Celebrated

The Mataeles, a large Tongan family, came to arrange for the burial of their wife and mother, who passed away at the age of ninety-four. I knew the condition of the body before I went to the arrangement office, and I was concerned that the family might not understand why this funeral would need to be closed casket. When I explained to the son that we would need to enclose the body in a container within the sealer casket, and that no one would be allowed to view her without signing a release absolving us of any blame in case of emotional distress, he immediately put my mind at ease by agreeing. He explained, "My mother was in the hospital on life support for two weeks. The doctor recommended removing life support because she was brain dead, but our father could not bear the thought of life without her. He hadn't slept for days. He was too tired to see what we saw: Her skin was starting to slip off of her, and her body was leaking. She was already gone." Throughout this painful conversation, the father, small in stature, remained silent and closed his eyes. He looked exhausted.

I felt for this family's loss, while at the same time I felt happy that they'd come to my mortuary. I loved to direct funeral services for traditional Tongan people. Indigenous to the South Pacific Islands, they had brought with them many beautiful customs when it came to laying loved ones to rest. Their evening services included singing their native songs and any number of planned or extemporaneous speeches. It was not uncommon for these services to last five or six hours. If the funeral director permitted it, the services would continue through the night. Guests brought gifts, often various lengths of lovely fabrics. Always, an abundance of food was served afterward. I seldom turned down an invitation to eat with them. They served four different kinds of meat, such as fried chicken, lobsters, roast beef, and pork from the pit. Rice was plentiful, three different kinds of bread or rolls, several kinds of salad, and wonderful desserts. It was a celebratory feast.

The service for Mrs. Mataele was held on Saturday morning at 10:00 a.m. in a large church. While setting up in the church the night before, it had been necessary for family members to remove two of the front pews to make room for the casket, which sat on woven grass mats with brightly colored fringes and was covered with white imported lace decorated with hand-stitched seed pearls. Personal items of the deceased and gifts surrounded the beautiful rose-colored casket, and the mats were covered with large tappa cloths made by natives pounding bark into thin sheets and drawing their native symbols on them with dark natural dyes.

The service ran overtime because of the many impromptu speeches. Just before the closing hymn, the husband decided he would speak. He talked in a quiet voice, stopping occasionally to cry into his handkerchief. He spoke in his native language so I didn't understand the exact words of his message, but I could tell from his great emotion that he was speaking of his long life with his departed wife. I felt deeply for his loss, which he was only just starting to comprehend.

It was common in Tongan funerals that all of the attendees would stay to watch the completion of the grave. Though I had alerted the cemetery employees of this ahead of time, they were running behind schedule; the sexton came by the site to say they were extra busy and it would be an hour before the men and heavy equipment could come to close the grave. The delay posed no problem to the Mataeles, who simply continued to sing their native songs in wonderful harmony. People continued to give spontaneous speeches about Mrs. Mataele. Someone in their group drove up in a blue pick-up truck that was carrying the body of a huge dead pig. The bristles had been removed, and it was ready to go into the pit in the ground to be cooked for dinner later. The pig lay on purple lace. Yellow lace was draped over the sides and cab of the truck. It was an amazing spectacle. People rushed to have their pictures taken with the pig before it was whisked away; when encouraged to join in, I had my picture taken with the pig, too, exchanging small talk with the family and friends and getting to know them better. I learned the backyard at their father's was set up with two huge tents, the floors of which were covered with rugs, mats, piles of folded bedding, and huge pillows for sitting and visiting. A large refrigerator had been brought in to keep food fresh for the crowd. Much of the cooking would be done on a barbecue. Some guests would stay for up to a week after the services, continuing to support the family in their grieving.

After a long wait, the grave was finally closed. Suddenly, the wizened old husband, who seemed to be reenergized, said he would like to hear from each of his twelve children. This event had brought them from many corners of the earth, and he wanted them to introduce their family members and tell the gathering what they were currently doing in their lives.

It was past four o'clock in the afternoon when they sang *God Be with You 'till We Meet Again*. They left the grave to go back to the family house for more singing, dancing, and the huge feast, which would last late into the night.

———

The Tongan families that I served often expressed their gratitude to me with delicious food and other gifts. I still cherish two tappa cloths, (one of which has royal symbols because the deceased was of royalty), two mats, a straw skirt, and a hand-appliquéd quilt with tribal patterns in purple on a white background.

I enjoyed how the Tongan funerals I worked on were such celebratory occasions. Yes, there was crying, but there was also a tremendous expression of love as they embraced and talked about the life of the loved one they had lost. The Tongan people always graciously extended their friendship to each other and to me. There was something truly transformative about the free expression of their feelings through song, speech, and physical embrace. Their approach to coping with death was a remarkable celebration of life.

Throughout my long career helping families mourn their loved ones, I was always intrigued by the many different ways that our respective cultures influence our approach to death. Traditional Muslims and Orthodox Jews refused embalming, which is considered to be a desecration of the body in those traditions. Buddhists and Hindus tended to choose cremation. Some cultures prefer elaborate caskets or mausoleums, while others insist on burying bodies directly into the earth. Depending on the cultures and the families themselves, some of the services I attended were quick and quiet, others long and wailing, and still others loud and celebratory.

Whether the funeral, memorial service, or a benediction at the final resting place lasts for minutes or hours, we all have a universal need to observe and respect a life lived. It is important that we express our own feelings as well as extend our sympathy and support to the survivors.

The need to grieve belongs to all mankind and even animals. Quails are known to be monogamous. Ed enjoyed feeding thirty of these beautiful birds in our backyard each evening. A mother quail flew into our large picture window and died immediately. I buried her. For more than a week, her mate hung around the yard calling often to her. He did not eat or drink. Then he flew helplessly into a block wall several times before dying on our lawn. Grief leaves all of us distraught. As humans, we have the unique ability to pause, to reflect, to acknowledge life, and to be reminded of our own mortal natures. In addition to our grief, death brings us the opportunity to reassess our own lives as well as our relationships so we can vow (maybe again) to make changes we see are needed.

Ultimately, our experience of someone's death is all relative to our relationship with the deceased, our age when the death occurs, the age of the deceased, and the nature of the death. And yet, no matter the circumstances or the inevitability of death, it almost always takes us by surprise. It is difficult for us to conceive of the hard-and-fast nature of mortality.

Working in the death care industry has shown me how very important it is that we all engage in our own dialogue on death. There is peace of mind in knowing what the other person wants. There is a feeling of relief in making our own desires known. Confronting this reality brings with it a kind of peace that denial never offers. It allows us to embrace life, in all its fleeting glory and suffering.

The Mortician Who Lost Her Husband

His name was Ed Nadle. He was my second husband. In 1995, he sold his die-casting business, persuaded me to retire, and we moved from our Hollywood, California home to retire in the beautiful red rock country of southwestern Utah near Zion's National Park. From there we traveled as we had long wished to Europe, Asia, South America, and Australia. We stopped only when Ed's health dictated it. He was eighty-nine years old when he was diagnosed with leukemia in 2001. Ed had a long history of cancer, so when word came of his latest relapse both of us knew his hopes were dim.

Early in our relationship we both acknowledged that life would end when our names were called so we had prepared for the inevitable. And by prepared I mean Ed had purchased his cemetery plot (when his first wife died in 1982), and I had purchased mine (while I was selling graves, I sold them to myself, eventually owning nine in three states). Ed had composed his will. So had I. He had even penned his own obituary.

But when the time came, I just wasn't ready.

A businessman by trade and planner by nature, Ed regarded the coming end with equanimity. Turned out it was I, so well trained in death, who found myself badly unprepared. Clinically, I knew what would happen to Ed's body. Emotionally, I was unsure what would happen to me. I was petrified at the prospect of life without the witty, broad-shouldered man who'd been my companion for eighteen years.

So much for my professional expertise: I felt like a physician who had never been ill.

Of course, by now, at the age of seventy-five, I had lived long enough to experience the deaths of friends and family. When my sister, Beth, died of complications from a stroke, I helped prepare her body. When my mother died, I styled her hair and did her makeup. I worked on my father's funeral arrangements, carrying on a family tradition of sorts—he had assisted with his own father's burial. His sisters had bathed and dressed their father while my father and his brothers dug the grave. The homemade casket was transported to the cemetery in a horse-drawn wagon.

But while these deaths all swept me up in sadness, they did not bring down the suffocating curtain of grief that enveloped me at the thought of Ed's almost-certain departure. My sister's stroke had left her in a vegetative state; her death struck me as a means of escape. The passing of my mother and father was mournful, but I saw it as a natural progression—an adult daughter parting with her elderly parents. I ached but I knew I would heal and go on.

Somehow Ed's death, and the loneliness it augured, nearly consumed me, even though I had much time to prepare. The doctor gave Ed two months to live, and Ed used all but three days of that allotment. It took one week for both of us to put an end to our anger. Ed was angry because he must leave a life filled with friends and family he loved deeply. Truthfully, under all my anger, I was afraid to be alone.

We talked and decided this would be the biggest change we had ever known—and who likes changes such as death brings? We planned to deal with the short time left to us by sending out word to his daughter and his five grandchildren of the doctor's prognosis. They organized and each family came separately, bringing their children and each visiting for three days. They were happy days, filled with laughter and tears. The smaller children played quiet games when they got bored with the nonstop conversation of the adults. Life was good for us, with Ed pausing for blood transfusions.

On the days we were free, we made short trips. We hadn't seen as much of scenic Utah as we wanted so we traveled towards the central part of the state as well as to canyons and parks we hadn't visited before.

After spending five days in the hospital, Ed sensed that the end was coming. He said, "Take me home, put me to sleep, and let's get this over with." He spent his last three days at our two-story brick home in St. George, Utah. At 11:00 p.m. on Ed's final night, the bulb in his bedside lamp went out. Three hours later, Ed did too. It happened quietly but the end was obvious.

Ed's funeral is one people will talk about for years. It was held in darkness.

As we left our home for the church on that Saturday in August, I noticed lightning in the north. Now, Ed was always known as a man in charge. It was never in a controlling manner but more as the born leader he was. His funeral service had just begun, and his granddaughter, Nancy, was beginning the eulogy when the lights went out. There was quiet laughter throughout the audience, along with sound of thunder outside. Those in attendance thought the same as I: Ed was in control to the very end. After the gospel message, the great- and the great-great-grandchildren sang, and I wished we had light so we could see those beautiful children. My thoughts were read because the lights came on for two seconds, then they remained off.

After stopping for lunch with friends at our home following the funeral service in St. George, our families drove six hours to Los Angeles, California. Ed was buried the next day after graveside services in the Forest Lawn Hollywood Hills Cemetery in a plot he had purchased twenty years before, next to the grave of his first wife, one of my dearest friends. After the funeral, our friends and family went about their lives. I went home to face a loneliness I had watched countless widows endure. But watching is one thing. Experiencing is another. I now know that there are some deaths we never get over. We only learn to live with them.

I live with good memories, many of them humorous. Our last trip was a cruise around the bottom tip of South America in 1999. We left the ship in Guatemala to see some ancient ruins. In order to reach them, we flew part way, took a bus part way, and walked five miles in the hot, humid jungle positioned near the equator.

Ed walked near the front of our group with a friend. I heard a man behind us say as he wiped the sweat running down his face. "I'll bet I'm the oldest one here. I'm seventy-four."

Ed's friend made the gentleman a ten-dollar bet. The good man paid the bet when Ed produced his driver's license showing he was eighty-seven years old. Then he inquired of my husband, "Aren't you afraid to travel like you do at your age?"

Ed responded, "I just bring my mortician with me."

As Madame de Staël so accurately said, "We understand death for the first time when he puts his hand upon one we love." Now that Ed is gone, I understand much more fully the experiences of the families I helped. I know better what they went through after my services ended. Their grief continued. So did their lives.

These days, I think a lot about the many good times of years past, and enjoy the good company of my cat, Purrcules. She weighs in at seventeen pounds and is a playful, well-behaved companion who demands little but food, a litter box, and the most comfortable spot in the house.

Life without Ed has become easier with the passing of time. For the past five years, it has been important that I keep my mind occupied. Writing and reading have been rewarding. So has hosting two young Armenian students as they complete their college degrees, taking breaks from their studies to keep me company, and cook traditional Armenian dinners. I volunteer in the public schools with young students who need a mentor to listen to them read. I belong to a book club, which keeps me with younger women and also a discussion group that places me with those my age. I travel to California several times a year to stay connected to my daughter Lorelle and to my grandchildren. My life is full, though I still grieve the loss of Ed in countless small ways and moments. Through it all, I continue to engage heartily in my own dialogue on death, even as the inevitable draws ever nearer.

About the Author

JUNE KNIGHTS NADLE graduated from the Cincinnati College of Mortuary Science in 1945 and began work in the mortuary business just after World War II, in an era when most women had few career options. Her career as a licensed funeral director and embalmer covered fifty years during which she worked in Los Angeles and Salt Lake City. She is now retired and lectures frequently on the topic of creating a dialogue with death to be better prepared for the inevitable. She lives in the beautiful red rock country of St. George, Utah, with her cat, Purrcules.